REDRAWING *the* MAP

The Partition of the Korean Peninsula

GERRY BOEHME

Cavendish Square
New York

Published in 2019 by Cavendish Square Publishing, LLC
243 5th Avenue, Suite 136, New York, NY 10016

First Edition

Library of Congress Cataloging-in-Publication Data

Names: Boehme, Gerry, author.
Title: The Partition of the Korean Peninsula / Gerry Boehme.
Description: First edition. | New York : Cavendish Square, 2019. | Series: Redrawing the map | Includes bibliographical references and index.
Identifiers: LCCN 2017059788 (print) | LCCN 2018000750 (ebook) | ISBN 9781502635785 (eBook) | ISBN 9781502635778 (library bound) | ISBN 9781502635792 (pbk.)
Subjects: LCSH: Korea--History--Partition, 1945--Juvenile literature. | Korean War, 1950-1953--Causes--Juvenile literature. | Korea--History--Juvenile literature.
Classification: LCC DS917.43 (ebook) | LCC DS917.43 .B64 2019 (print) | DDC 951.904/1--dc23
LC record available at https://lccn.loc.gov/2017059788

Editorial Director: David McNamara
Editor: Erin L. McCoy
Copy Editor: Michele Suchomel-Casey
Associate Art Director: Amy Greenan
Designer: Jessica Nevins
Production Coordinator: Karol Szymczuk
Photo Research: J8 Media

The photographs in this book are used by permission and through the courtesy of: Cover Photo 12/Alamy Stock Photo; p. 4 Serban Bogdan/Shutterstock.com; p. 8 Ed Jones/AFP/Getty Images; p. 10 Topical Press Agency/Hulton Archive/Getty Images; p. 13 Chris 73/Wikimedia Commons/File:Three Kingdoms of Korea Map pl.png/CC BY-SA 3.0; p. 18 Amble/Wikimedia Commons/File:Ganghwa location.svg/CC BY-SA 3.0; pp. 22-23, 33, 36 Universal Images Group/Getty Images; p. 27 Historicair/Wikimedia Commons/File:Tsushima battle map-en.svg/CC BY-SA 3.0; p. 31 Bureau d'information coréen/Wikimedia Commons/File:L'Indépendance de la Corée et la Paix-04.jpg/CCO; p. 34 George Strock/The LIFE Picture Collection/Getty Images; p. 39 Howard Sochurek/The LIFE Picture Collection/Getty Images; p. 45 Kyodo News/Getty Images; pp. 46-47 Handout/Getty Images; p. 51 Rishabh Tatiraju/Wikimedia Commons/ File:Korea DMZ.svg/CC BY-SA 3.0; p. 57 Universal History Archive/Universal Images Group/Getty Images; pp. 59, 67 Bettmann/Getty Images; p. 69 Bert Hardy/Picture Post/Getty Images; p. 71 Interim Archives/Archive Photos/Getty Images; pp. 76-77 Peter Hermes Furian/Shutterstock.com; p. 79 Nathan Benn/Corbis Historical/Getty Images; p. 81 Diana Walker/The LIFE Images Collection/Getty Images; pp. 82, 83 Keystone-France/Gamma-Keystone/Getty Images; p. 87 Amble and Tomchen1989/Wikimedia Commons/File:Map of Korean maritime border.svg/CC BY-SA 3.0; p. 91 Roman Babakin/Shutterstock.com; p. 93 STR/AFP/Getty Images; p. 96 Pool/Getty Images.

Printed in the United States of America

CONTENTS

ZEMLYA
NEW SIBERIAN ISLANDS
Wrangel Island
Khatanga
Tiksi
Allaykba
Ambarchik
Igarka
Olenek
Zhigansk
Stradnekolymsk
Anadyr
Oymyakon
Kamenskoye
USSIA
Yakutsk
Olekminsk
Okhotsk
Krasnoyarsk
Irkutsk
Nikolayevsk
Petropavlovsk
Ulan Bator
MONGOLIA
Harbin
Urumchi
Sapporo
Vladivostok
Mukden
NORTH KOREA
Beijing
P'yongyang
Tientsin
JAPAN
Taiyuan
Seoul
CHINA
SOUTH KOREA
Nagoya
Tokyo
Kyoto
Suchow
Osaka
NORTH
PACIFIC
OCEAN
Shanghai
Chengou
Wu-han
NEPAL
Lhasa
BHUTAN
Nan-chang
Thimphu
Kunming
Foochow
BANGLADESH
Taipei
Calcutta
Canton
MYANMAR (BURMA)
Hong Kong
Luang Prabang
LAOS
Aparri
Rangoon
Baguro
THAILAND
Manila
Bangkok
VIETNAM
ADAMAN ISLANDS (INDIA)
CAMBODIA
PHILIPPINES
GUAM
NICOBAR ISLANDS (INDIA)
FEDERATED STATES OF MICRONESIA
Davao
MARSHALL ISLANDS
Pinang
BRUNEI
MALAYSIA
Medan
Kuala Lumpur
Singapore
Djambi
Palembang
Bandjarmasin
Jayapura
KIRIB
Jakarta
INDONESIA
PAPUA NEW GUINEA
Rabaul
SOLOMON ISLANDS
Semarang
Surabaja
Port Moresby
TUVALU
Darwin
Cooktown
Wyndham
VANUATU
FIJI
Broome
Burketown
Townsville
TONGA
Port Hedland
NEW CALEDONIA (FRANCE)
Rockhampton
IAN
EAN
Carnarvon
AUSTRALIA
Brisbane
Geraldton
Perth
Port Augusta
Newcastle
Sydney
Port Lincoln
Adelaide
Wollongong
Albany
Canberra
Auckland
Melbourne
Launceston
Wellington
NEW ZEALAND
Hobart
TASMANIA (AUSTRALIA)
Timaru
Dunedin

CHAPTER ONE

A People Divided

On November 12, 2017, people around the world watched with amazement as a North Korean soldier braved a hail of bullets to escape to South Korea. North Korean guards shot the unarmed man as he ran toward the joint security area (JSA), a section of the demilitarized zone (DMZ) that separates the northern half of the Korean peninsula from the south. Luckily, the soldier survived, becoming one of the few North Koreans to successfully cross the line that divides the peninsula.

Just one week later, on November 20, American president Donald Trump placed North Korea back on the United States government's list of state sponsors of terrorism. His action represented yet another attempt to force North Korea to stop developing nuclear weapons that could threaten both South Korea and the world.

Opposite: North and South Korea lie on a peninsula that occupies a strategic position between China and Japan.

From One People

Today, it would be difficult to find two countries more different than South Korea and North Korea. South of the 38th parallel lies an energetic and prosperous democracy, devoted to freedom and individual rights. North of the line sits an austere, repressive state viewed by most other countries as a dangerous, rogue nation with no respect for international laws.

However, North and South Korea actually share the same history and culture, and the Korean people lived as one nation for more than a thousand years. All of the differences that we observe between the two nations today stem from just one event: the arbitrary partition of the Korean peninsula after World War II.

A Strategic Position

Foreign empires have attempted to dominate the Korean peninsula throughout its history. The Chinese, the Mongols, the Russians, the Japanese—all have looked to control Korea for its natural resources and its strategic location on the Asian continent. The

A COMMON HERITAGE

Despite their political separation, North and South Koreans still share a common ethnic heritage, and Koreans have traditionally been taught to take pride in their homogeneity. While immigration to South Korea has recently increased, non-Koreans still account for less than 4 percent of its population.

long coastlines along its eastern and western shores, its proximity to the Pacific Ocean and Japan, and its common borders with China and Russia have all played a major role in shaping the peninsula's fate.

While Korea shares a long and complex history with China, its neighbor to the north, it managed to avoid significant, extended contact with other nations until the late 1800s. Since that time, Korea has often suffered as a pawn on a global chessboard controlled by international powers.

When Japan annexed Korea in 1910, it began to plant the seeds for the two different Koreas we see today. Not only did Japan steal the peninsula's resources and enslave its people, it also robbed Koreans of their culture and national identity. Japan's defeat in World War II ended its occupation of Korea, but by that point, the victorious Allies showed signs of their own divisions between democracy and Communism—the same type of division that would split the Korean peninsula in two.

Rather than risk a new war over Korea, in 1945 the United States and the Soviet Union decided to temporarily split the peninsula along a purely arbitrary line, the 38th parallel. The division happened so quickly that many Koreans found themselves separated from their families and friends, never to be seen or heard from again.

After the partition, the United States and the Soviet Union moved quickly to form governments and choose leaders that conformed to their own respective

Minefields and barbed wire mark the demilitarized zone (DMZ) that separates South and North Korea.

ideologies: democratic in the south and Communist in the north. The border has changed little since that time, even after an armistice ended a bloody war between North and South Korea that lasted from 1950 to 1953 and involved other nations, including the United States and China.

Only a Dream

Today, North and South Korea continue to face one another over a dividing line that bisects the demilitarized zone, which has been described as the most dangerous place on earth, lined with razor-wire fences and more than a million landmines, and defended by more than one million combat-ready troops. Despite the danger, tourists and South Koreans can visit the DMZ, and it ranks as one of the most popular places to see in South Korea.

Many Koreans still hope that, some day, their two countries will once again be reunited. However, given the current crisis over North Korea's nuclear program and continued hostility between north and south, it's difficult to imagine that the suffering that has resulted from this division could ever end in our lifetime. The "temporary" border between South and North Korea looks to be more permanent than ever.

CHAPTER TWO

Caught Between Nations

Koreans have always taken great pride in their homeland. Ever since the first people came to settle on the peninsula thousands of years ago, Koreans have fiercely guarded both their lands and their cultural heritage from invaders and outside influences.

Unfortunately, Koreans could not always successfully resist those who desired control over their citizens and resources. Korea's history shows both long stretches of unity, peace, and prosperity mixed with other periods during which foreign powers dominated the peninsula.

Even in difficult times, however, Koreans remained determined to throw off outside rulers and return to self-rule. The very thought that their homeland could exist as two separate nations would have seemed impossible to Koreans until other countries divided the

Opposite: Japanese policemen enforced their country's occupation of Korea from 1910 until the end of World War II.

peninsula at the end of World War II. This partition introduced Koreans to a new, cruel reality that would result in more than seventy years of conflict and suffering.

Land of Legend

Korea is one of the oldest countries in the world. Archaeologists believe that prehistoric people probably migrated from Siberia, Manchuria, and Mongolia to Korea. The ancestors of modern-day Koreans may have moved to the area as long ago as 6000 BCE.

When Koreans describe the origins of their homeland, they often recite the legend of Hwanung, the son of the Lord of Heaven, who came to earth to live on a volcano on the northern border of Korea, transformed a bear into a beautiful woman, and married her. Their son, Tangun, became the father of Korea.

History does indeed record a leader named Tangun (also known as Dangun) who established Korea's first kingdom, Old Choson (the "Land of the Morning Calm," also called ancient Joseon or Gojoseon) in 2333 BCE. In fact, South Korea still honors its first leader each year on October 3, National Foundation Day.

A Series of Kingdoms

Korea's written history began when the Chinese Han dynasty occupied four territories in northern Korea

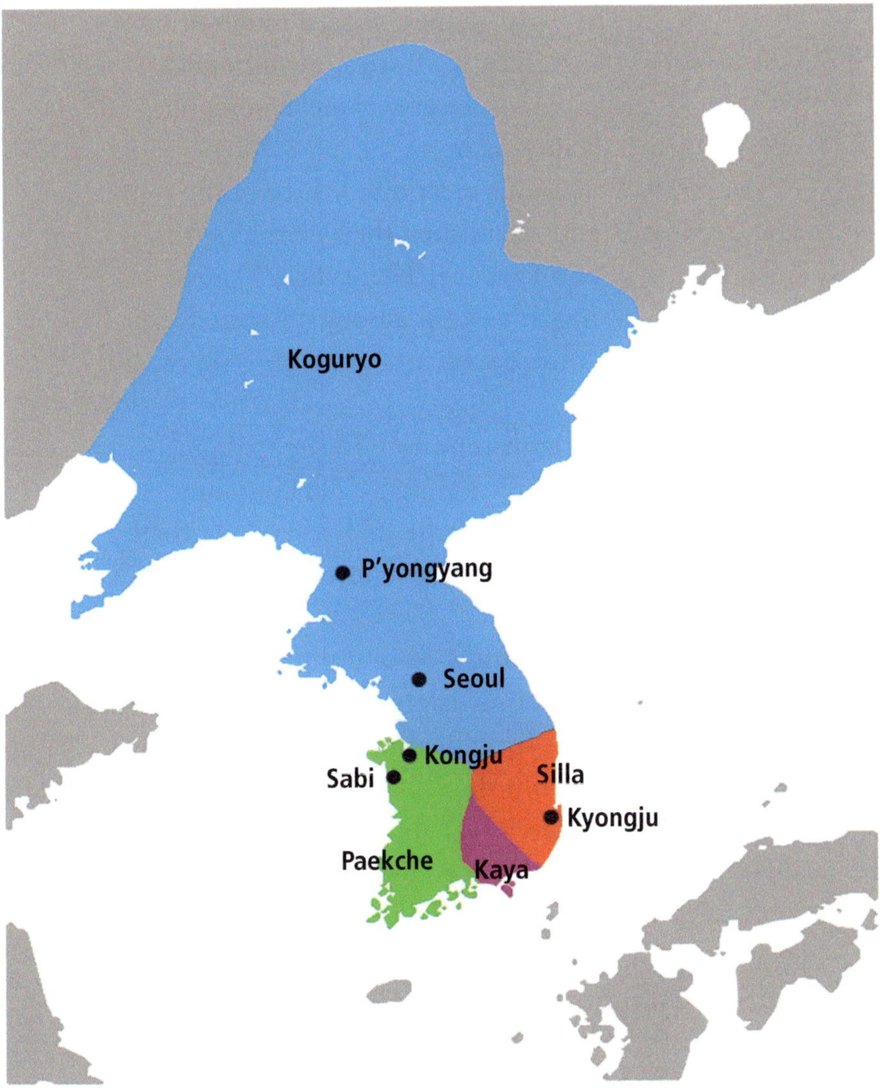

Three kingdoms and the confederation of Kaya controlled the Korean peninsula until the seventh century, by which time Silla had absorbed Koguryo and Paekche as well as Kaya.

in 108 BCE. The early Chinese passed much of their culture on to the Korean territories, including their written language, system of government, religion, and the use of metals such as iron.

In 75 BCE, Koreans recaptured three of the four Han territories and established their own kingdoms: Silla, Koguryo, and Paekche. These three Korean kingdoms then began to fight amongst themselves, presenting the Chinese with an opportunity to regain their influence.

During the seventh century CE, the Chinese Tang dynasty helped the stronger Silla kingdom conquer Koguryo and Paekche. However, Silla then turned against China and took control over the entire Korean peninsula.

Arts and culture flourished under the Silla kingdom's reign; this time is often referred to as Korea's golden age. Koreans simplified the system of writing they had adopted from the Chinese, and a local literature quickly developed and spread. These years also witnessed advances in architecture and skilled crafts such as ironware, ceramics, and jewelry.

In the late eighth century, Silla noblemen began fighting amongst themselves for supremacy in the kingdom. In 918, a leader named Wang Kon finally gained control and called his new kingdom Koryo, a shorter version of Koguryo. The name "Koryo" eventually became the "Korea" we know today.

Over the years, Koryo's power weakened as foreign kingdoms, including Japan and China, continued to raid its territory. In 1231, the Mongols invaded Korea, taking control of much of the peninsula. The Mongols' power eventually declined, however, leaving Korea ready to be unified again.

Five Centuries of Stability

In 1392, General Yi Seong-gye, a supporter of the Ming dynasty in China, led a largely peaceful takeover of Koryo and formed the New Choson dynasty.

Compared to its earlier history, the Choson dynasty marked a remarkably long period of relative peace, stability, and independence for the Korean peninsula. The dynasty ruled Korea for more than five hundred years, from 1392 to 1910. Confucian teachings adopted from China formed the basis of government, and General Yi moved the capital city to Hanyang, the present-day location of South Korea's capital city of Seoul. Many aspects of Korean culture flourished, including technology, science, and music.

Trouble with Foreign Powers

During the long reign of the New Choson dynasty, its leaders tried to isolate their kingdom from any outside contact, tending to trade only with China on their northern border. However, Korea's attempts to seal itself off from the rest of the world did not stop its neighbors from lusting after its lands and resources. The Mongols continued to push into Korea, and Japan frequently attacked cities on the eastern coast.

Japan launched a full-scale invasion of Korea in 1592. Not only did the Japanese want Korea for themselves, they also viewed the peninsula as the perfect launching pad to mount an invasion of China. Despite fierce Korean resistance, Japan successfully captured many Korean cities, including Busan, Seoul, and P'yongyang in the north. After a brief truce in 1596, Japan invaded again in 1597.

The Chinese recognized the threat that Japan posed to their own border with Korea. With Chinese help, the Koreans finally managed to drive Japan off their peninsula in 1598. The struggle left Korea weak, however, and its former ally, China, then tried to expand its own presence.

China maintained its strong influence on Korea through the end of the nineteenth century. Korea paid high amounts of tribute to China to keep its independence, but China's protection also helped Korea gain some measure of peace and stability. During that time, however, Koreans also became increasingly convinced that foreign influence led to nothing but trouble, and they took even stronger steps than they had in the past to isolate themselves from any outside contact. For many years Korea enforced laws that severely limited interaction with any country other than China.

European Pressure

The situation began to change for the worse toward the end of the 1800s, when the Korean peninsula got caught in the middle of a swirl of international competition and conflict that would change its history forever.

In the eighteenth and nineteenth centuries, the Industrial Revolution sent countries all over the world in search of new raw materials to be used for manufacturing and new markets to sell their goods. Foreign countries, including Great Britain, France, Russia, and the United States, soon became interested in gaining influence in this strange, unknown country they knew as "Choson." They especially wanted access to its natural resources, which included coal and iron. Not only did these countries wish to benefit by establishing trade relationships with Korea, they also feared that their rivals could gain a competitive advantage if they managed to gain their own control.

At first, Korea tried to resist all contact with these foreigners. In fact, Choson came to be known as the "Hermit Kingdom" due to its insistence on cutting itself off from the rest of the world. The Westerners could not be deterred, however; they continued to force their presence on the Korean peninsula. Some of their attempts resulted in short but bloody armed conflicts with Korean defenders.

Confrontation

In 1866, the French attacked Kanghwa Island off the northwest coast of Korea, near present-day Inchon, after Korea executed a number of French Catholic priests and their followers. Korean forces managed

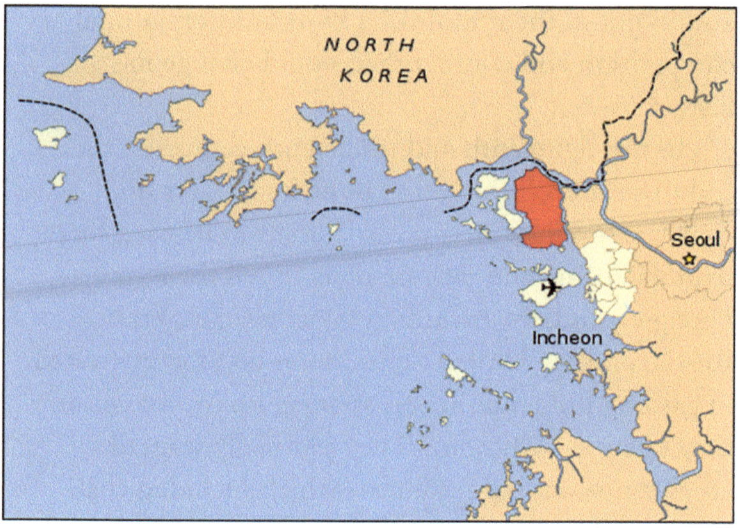

Korea resisted foreign intervention at Kanghwa Island several times in the late 1800s. The island still holds a strategic position today.

to drive the attackers away after a brief battle. That same year, an American ship attempted to sail up the Taedong River to P'yongyang to establish trade relations, but the ship ran aground and Koreans burned it and killed all aboard.

The United States Navy returned in May of 1871, but Korean forces refused to allow its ships to sail past Kanghwa Island and upriver toward Seoul. Fighting broke out, and nearly three hundred Koreans were killed. US forces even occupied the island for a short time before leaving.

Despite these and other incidents, Korea still successfully limited its contact with other nations for another five years. The situation changed drastically in 1876, however, when Japan decided to force its own trade agreement upon Korea. Japan's attempt at trade resulted directly from lessons it had itself recently learned from Europe and America.

Lessons from the West

As Western powers began to increase their presence in the Far East in the 1800s, Japan mirrored its Korean neighbor and became increasingly isolationist in its own right. Before 1852, Japan severely limited its contact with the West and forbade most westerners from setting foot on Japanese soil.

In 1853, Commodore Matthew C. Perry of the United States Navy commanded his squadron to enter Tokyo Bay and force the Japanese to establish relations with America. One year later, the United States pressured Japan to sign the Convention of Kanagawa, a treaty that opened Japanese ports to US trade.

Japan bitterly resented that it was not strong enough to prevent a foreign power from getting its way. Japan had already seen Western nations force China to bend to their will. While the island nation had tried to prevent Europe and the United States from entering its own country, Perry's visit and the subsequent treaty proved to the Japanese that they had better adopt a new philosophy if they hoped to survive and grow as a powerful nation in their own right.

Shortly after signing the Convention of Kanagawa, Japan began to reform its government, strengthen its military, and modernize local industry. After watching Europe and America use superior force to occupy foreign lands and establish colonies to enrich themselves, the Japanese decided that they, too, wanted to become a world power, and they planned their first steps to establish their own empire in Asia.

Their first target? The Korean peninsula.

It had been nearly three centuries since Japan had launched a full-scale invasion of Korea. Japan now determined that the time was right to, once again, move against its closest neighbor across the strait.

Japan in Korea

Japan had several reasons for wanting to take control of Korea. Japan was working hard to expand its industry but had few natural resources. Korea, on the other hand, possessed rich and abundant resources such as coal, iron, and forests that could help build and fuel Japan's new factories. In addition, China and the nations of the West were already showing their own interest in Korea, and Japan worried that the peninsula could soon fall under the control of foreign powers and possibly threaten Japan itself with invasion.

Japan planned to copy what Europeans had done so successfully when they established colonies in the Americas, Asia, the Middle East, and Africa. The island nation aspired to control all of the Far East, and it intended to use Korea as a staging ground to move by land into China, Mongolia, and beyond.

So in 1875, Japan sent a ship to explore the Korean coast. Like the French and Americans before them, the Japanese chose to approach Kanghwa Island, where a fort guarded the mouth of the river that led to Seoul, the capital city. The Koreans forced the Japanese to withdraw after firing on their ship and on the soldiers who were attempting to land there.

Early the following year, the Japanese decided to employ the same tactics that US admiral Perry had demonstrated in Tokyo Bay just a few years earlier. They sent a large naval force to Korea and insisted that the kingdom sign a treaty that would open Korea to Japanese trade.

China now felt threatened by Japan's rising influence on the peninsula. Hoping to maintain its own position and dilute Japan's power, China encouraged Korea to open up its relations with other countries as well. Within ten years, Korea had signed additional trade agreements with the United States, Great Britain, and Russia. Meanwhile, competition for control of the peninsula mounted.

This sudden and increasing foreign presence prompted a backlash among Koreans and sparked a struggle for political control. In 1882, the Korean king and queen managed to suppress a peasant revolt with help from Chinese troops. Two years later, Japan supported a revolt that overthrew the royal family; Japan, in turn, was defeated with aid from Chinese soldiers.

A Foreign Battleground

The situation came to a head in 1894, and the Korean peninsula would never be the same.

The Japanese defeated China in the first Sino-Japanese War in 1894–1895 and took control of Korea.

A massive protest by Korean peasants against poor living conditions, government corruption, and foreign influence soon turned violent. After a peasant army defeated government forces, the Korean king once again asked China for help. The introduction of Chinese troops violated a previous treaty between China and Japan, providing the Japanese with the excuse they needed; in the summer of 1894, Japan moved its own troops into Korea to defend its interests.

After Japan attacked and defeated Chinese forces near Seoul, the two countries officially declared war on August 1, marking the beginning of the first Sino-Japanese War. While most of the world expected the larger Chinese army to win easily, what happened was exactly the opposite.

Japan had modernized its army with better equipment, planning, and training, and it quickly overwhelmed Chinese forces on the Korean peninsula. By March 1895, the Japanese had successfully advanced north to Manchuria and threatened the Chinese capital of Beijing, forcing the Chinese to seek peace. The war ended with the Treaty of Shimonoseki, in which China ceded control of Korea and gave some of its own territory, including the island of Taiwan, to Japan.

Japan Moves In

The Treaty of Shimonoseki granted Korea independence from Chinese control. However, Japan simply replaced China as a strong foreign power

CHINA'S INFLUENCE

China influenced Korean politics and culture for nearly one thousand years before the Japanese occupation. When World War II ended, Russia and the United States determined Korea's fate, but the Korean War would present China with its next opportunity to dominate the peninsula.

looking to exploit Korea for its own purposes. Even worse, Japan's plans for Korea would prove to be far more sinister than anything China had done.

As soon as the war ended, Japan took steps to modernize Korea in the same way it had transformed its own country to compete with the West. Government authority shifted from the king and queen to officials who reformed Korea's government and eliminated much of the country's traditional class and social structure. Korea's Queen Min, who had previously resisted Japan with the help of China in 1882, now renewed her opposition. With China out of the picture, the queen secretly reached out to Russia for help. In retaliation, Queen Min was murdered by the Japanese in 1895.

Fearing for his life, her husband, King Kojong, abandoned the royal palace and fled to the Russian diplomatic mission, where he tried to rule Korea under Russian supervision. After hearing that Koreans might be ready to revolt against all foreign control, the king returned to his palace in 1897. His reign would be short-lived.

THE BATTLE OF TSUSHIMA

Throughout its history the Korean peninsula and its surrounding waters have served as battlegrounds for warring neighbor nations. Such was the case in 1905, when Japan's navy destroyed a Russian fleet during a battle that took place in Korea's Tsushima Strait.

When the Russo-Japanese War began in 1904, Japan wanted to control the seas around Korea to support its troops on the peninsula and in Manchuria. For its part, Russia knew that it needed naval superiority to disrupt Japanese supply lines. Russia decided to strengthen its naval forces by moving ships from its fleet in the faraway Baltic Sea to the Pacific.

To join the fight against Japan, these Russian reinforcements had to sail 18,000 miles (28,968 kilometers) around Africa, across the Indian Ocean and past Southern Asia. As they finally approached the Yellow Sea, Russia ordered its fleet to proceed to its port at Vladivostok.

There were two ways to get there. The Russians could either sail to the east around Japan, or they could pass through the Tsushima Strait.

The Korea Strait connects the East China Sea to the Sea of Japan. The Tsushima Islands split the Korea Strait into two narrow passages: the Tsushima Strait to the east, which separates the Tsushima Islands and the Japanese islands of Kyushu and Honshu, and the western channel (or Choson Strait), which runs between the islands and the south coast of the Korean peninsula.

Admiral Zinovy Rozhestvensky, the commander of the Russian fleet, decided to steam through the Tsushima Strait to reach the Sea of Japan. Admiral Togo Heihachiro, the Japanese commander, correctly predicted the Russians' route and set his ships in ambush.

During the vicious battle that took place from May 27–29, 1905, Japan virtually destroyed the Russian fleet and convinced Russia's leaders to seek peace.

The Battle of Tsushima became the first great naval battle of the twentieth century. It badly damaged Russia's international reputation while establishing Japan's rise as a naval power. More important, Japan's victory paved the way for its occupation of the Korean peninsula.

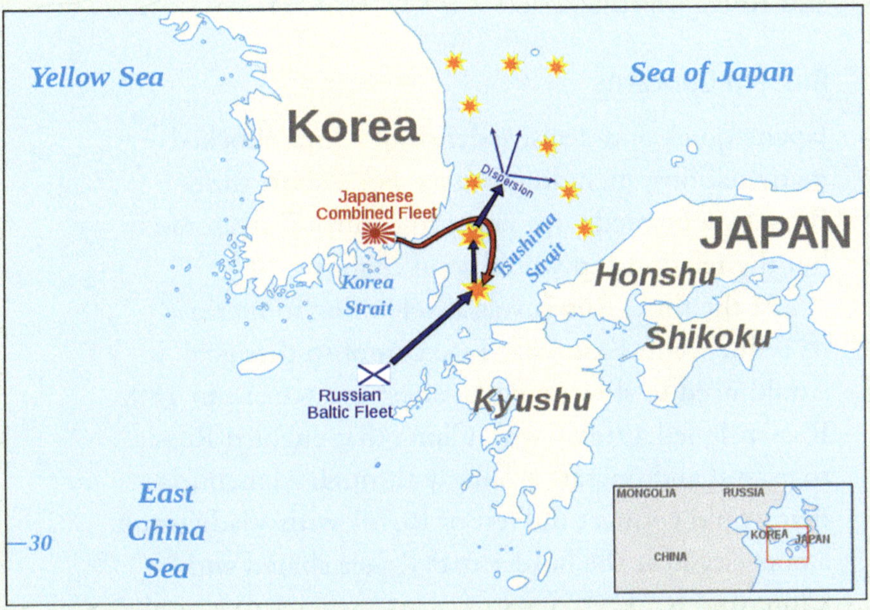

The Japanese navy shattered the Russian Baltic fleet during the Battle of Tsushima off the Korean coast in 1905. Japan's victory established its position as a great naval power and helped it gain total control of Korea.

Japan and Russia had already discussed cooperating to control Korea and possibly even splitting the peninsula in half. Both countries now teamed up to force King Kojong to grant them concessions: Russia gained rights to Korea's forests, while Japan wrested control of businesses and banks. Other countries also took advantage of Korea's weakness to assure their own access to Korean assets. This included the United States, which managed to take control of gold mines, railroads, and electrical power systems.

Nations of the world were having a feeding frenzy, and Korea was the prize.

Russian Concerns

Japan's quick and decisive defeat of China shocked many nations, including Russia. For a short time, Russia cooperated with Japan to control Korean assets, but the relationship would soon change.

At the time, Russia was also looking to increase its influence in East Asia. To accomplish that goal, it would need to slow down Japanese growth. So in 1896, Russia signed a treaty with China that enabled Russia to extend and operate a railway through Manchuria that would connect the rest of Russia with Vladivostok, a port city near the border that Russia shared with China and Korea.

For its part, Japan felt that Russia's cooperation with China in the region threatened its position in the peninsula. Even more concerning, a Russian invasion of Korea might leave the Japanese mainland vulnerable to a Russian attack. In 1903, Japan demanded that Russia remove its troops from Manchuria. When Russia refused, Japan responded aggressively.

The Russo-Japanese War broke out on February 8, 1904, when the Imperial Japanese Navy launched a surprise attack on the Russian fleet outside Port Arthur in Manchuria. After a string of Japanese victories on land and sea, the war effectively ended with another convincing Japanese naval victory in the Tsushima Strait, located at the lower right of the Korean peninsula between Korea and Japan.

In the treaty that ended the Russo-Japanese War in 1905, Russia recognized Japan's "paramount political, military and economic interest" in Korea. US president Theodore Roosevelt won the Nobel Peace Prize for helping negotiate the treaty; the United States also agreed to give Japan free reign in Korea and Manchuria as long as it would not interfere with American control of the Philippines, which had become a US territory after the Spanish-American War.

In the space of just more than a decade, Japan had fought and won two major wars against its rivals in the region. The entire world took notice; Japan's victory over Russia marked the first instance in modern times in which a country from Asia had defeated one from Europe. These convincing victories over two world powers left Japan dominant in Asia and, sadly for Koreans, over their homeland in particular. Once again, other nations had come together to determine Korea's fate.

The Japanese Occupation

Possession of Korea now gave Japan the resources and the geographic advantage it needed to launch attacks into China and Russia while defending its homeland. Japan's first step was to take control of the entire Korean peninsula. In 1905, Japan made Korea a protectorate. The latter still had its own ruler but, in reality, Japan controlled the government. Five years later, Japan dropped all pretenses and took total possession of Korea, making it a colony of the Japanese empire.

Japan's annexation of Korea marked the first stage of what was to become decades of cruel exploitation, leaving in its wake memories that still haunt Korean relations with Japan today.

An Assault Against Culture

Not only did Japan strip Korea of its rights as an independent nation and take control of its territory and resources, Japan also took steps to tear the heart out of local culture and erase Korea's unique identity from the earth.

Almost immediately, Japanese citizens seized Korean businesses and farmland. They also took control of all the peninsula's natural resources and built railroads, ports, and dams. While Japan certainly helped to modernize Korea after centuries of isolation, it acted for its own benefit, not for the good of Koreans.

The attack on Korean heritage and culture was just as savage. Japan forbade the Korean language from being

After the Japanese took control of Korea, they erected barricades to prevent Korean demonstrations demanding independence.

spoken or taught in schools. Koreans had to assume Japanese names and practice Japanese rituals. The Japanese stole Korean art and forced millions of Korean people to work as laborers, little more than slaves.

After centuries of independent rule and isolation from other countries, Koreans had been robbed of their heritage and now lived as subjects to a foreign power in their own country.

Still Dreaming of Independence

Early on in the occupation, Koreans tried to attract world attention and gain international recognition for their homeland as an independent state. In 1919, a Korean delegation traveled to France to attend the peace conference that ended World War I in order to ask the victorious Allied forces for their support. When they failed, millions of Koreans back home took part in demonstrations to demand their freedom.

Japan moved quickly and cruelly to suppress these and other demonstrations under what Koreans called Samil, or the March First Movement. After Japan killed more than seventy-five hundred Koreans and arrested more than forty-six thousand, the movement collapsed. Koreans still honor these victims by celebrating March 1 as a national holiday across the peninsula—one of the few things that both North and South Korea agree on today.

Although the March First Movement failed, it did help to create a resistance government, the Korean Provisional Government, which based itself in Shanghai, China. It also fueled the popularity of the Korean Communist Party.

Enduring World War II

In 1937, Japan and China went to war. Just as planned, Japan immediately used Korea as a bridge to invade China. When the United States entered the war against Japan after the bombing of Pearl Harbor in 1941, Korean men were forced to join the Imperial Japanese Army or work as slave laborers. By 1944, more than four million Koreans had been forced to move out of their country, with many being sent to Japan.

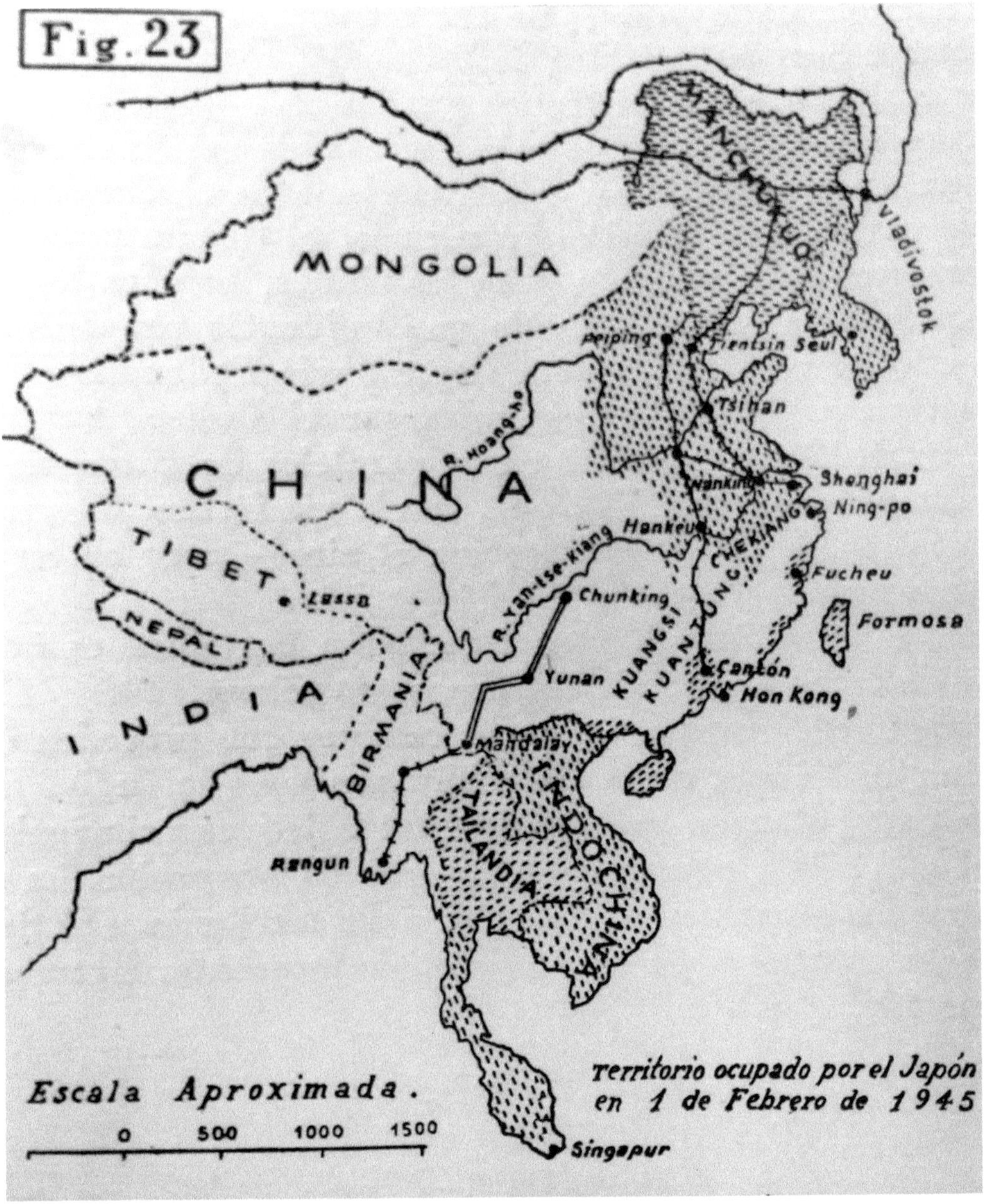

At the height of its power during World War II, Japan expanded its empire to control Korea, Southeast Asia, and part of China.

During World War II, the Japanese forced many Koreans to work as slave laborers. Many survivors were rescued by Allied forces.

Korean women, children, and the elderly worked in factories to build weapons, ships, and planes for the Japanese. Korean women suffered even further indignity by being kidnapped and forced to serve as prostitutes in brothels that Japan set up for its soldiers all over Asia.

When World War II ended with the defeat of Japan, the Korean people initially rejoiced in the hope that the cruel occupation would end and that foreign forces would finally leave their soil. But a new brand of hostility arose to take its place. Japan and Germany may have been defeated, but the victorious Allies now faced their own crisis. The Cold War—the battle between democracy and Communism—was about to begin. Once again, the Korean people would be victimized in another power struggle between foreign nations.

This time, however, the Korean people would be pitted against their own sisters and brothers across a new, artificial border.

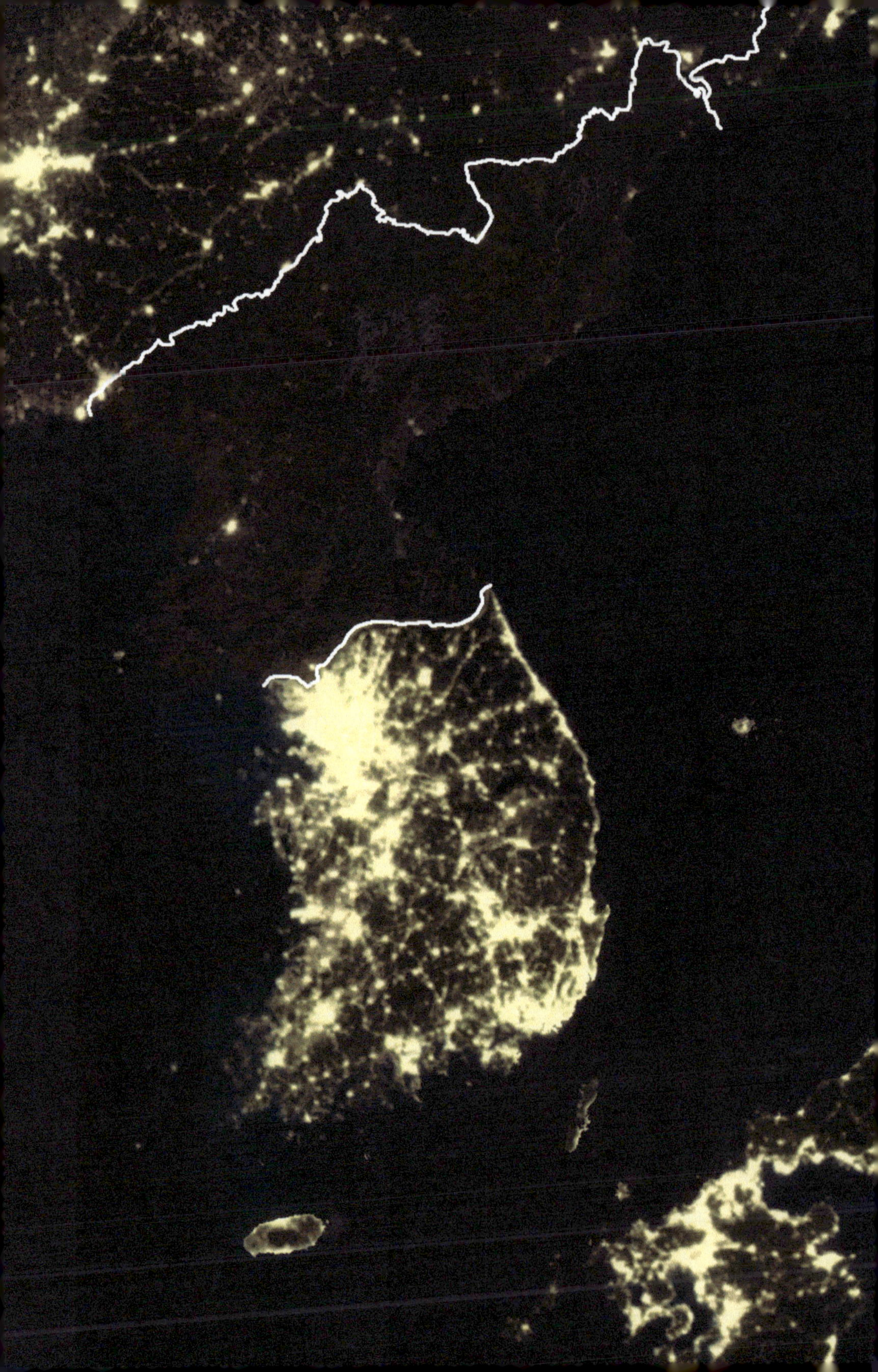

CHAPTER THREE

A Natural Bridge

When real estate agents describe the three most important factors in determining a home's value, they often use an old saying: "location, location, location." These agents know that, while people can remodel or rebuild a home, they usually can't move it. Therefore, much of a home's value depends upon where it was constructed and the land upon which it sits. Is the house located in a good neighborhood, close to stores and schools? Does it have great views? Is it close to water?

Like homes, nations also derive both advantages and disadvantages from their geographic location. Some countries possess valuable natural resources like minerals, coal, and oil. Others border rivers and oceans with access to international trade routes. Still more lie in strategic locations that connect one group of people

Opposite: The Korean peninsula is surrounded by oceans and offers great mineral wealth. In this satellite image from 2012, urban and industrial centers are lit up, and a sharp contrast between North and South Korea is visible.

with another or possess natural barriers that offer protection against unwanted visitors. Few countries, however, possess all of the above.

Korea happens to be one of those few. It holds a strategically important position near the midpoint of the Asian continent's eastern coast. Surrounded by oceans and boasting mountains covered in forests and filled with valuable minerals, Korea has long been envied by its neighbors for its natural resources and location.

More than any other factor, Korea's geography has played a major role in shaping the history of its people. For thousands of years, Koreans have been forced to defend themselves against encroachment by foreign powers. They often use the proverb, "When whales fight, the shrimp's back is broken," to describe how their country has been subjected to attacks and exploitation from its more powerful neighbors.

Korea shares most of its northern land border with China, so it may come as no surprise that China has exerted more influence on Korea than any other nation.

Korea and China share a checkered history of war and cooperation. Even during many centuries of relative peace, Korea was often forced to make payments to the Chinese court and acknowledge the authority of the Chinese emperor over the Korean king. In return, Korea received trade, protection, and control over its internal affairs.

Close, prolonged contact with China influenced Korea in other ways as well. Over the course of time,

Many of Korea's social and political practices have been shaped by the teachings of Chinese philosopher Confucius (*shown above in red*).

many aspects of Chinese society worked their way into Korea's culture. Korea's written language is derived from Chinese characters, and much of its social philosophy is based on the teachings of Confucius, a Chinese teacher, politician, and philosopher who lived from 551 to 479 BCE.

Confucianism provides a model for personal behavior that defines how people, and even nations, interact with one another. Its primary purpose is to achieve harmony internally and with others, and it strongly emphasizes values that include a social order and the acceptance of responsibilities. In Confucian culture, all people are expected to adopt well-defined roles and act "properly" in all aspects of their life.

While North and South Korea certainly live under vastly different political systems today, they continue to share certain social customs that trace their roots back to Chinese Confucian teachings. In many ways, both North and South Korea still practice elements of *li*, the "proper way." Both countries preach personal control of emotions, obedience to authority, accepting one's role, and conforming to social norms.

A Desirable Territory

While Korea's historical relationship with China has been complex, to say the least, its dealings with other nations in the region follow a simpler pattern, based mostly on confrontation. In addition to the Chinese,

Koreans have also fought the Japanese, Mongols, Russians, and other nations to protect their homeland. In some instances, Koreans have been forced to stand to the side and watch these same nations fight amongst themselves, on Korean soil, for control of the peninsula so that they could expand their own empires.

Why was Korea so desirable? In many ways, the same geographical features that made Korea such a difficult place to invade also made it an attractive target for conquest.

The Korean peninsula juts out about 680 miles (1,100 km) into the Pacific Ocean from the eastern Asian continent. Its 84,402 square miles (218,600 sq km) are surrounded on three sides by water: the Korea Bay and the Yellow Sea to the west, the Korea Strait to the south, and the Sea of Japan to the east.

Mountains blanket most of the peninsula's interior, especially in the north. In fact, today's North Korea stands out as one of the most mountainous nations in the world.

For most of its history, steep mountains, narrow valleys, and jagged coasts made it difficult for invading armies to attack and occupy the peninsula. On the other hand, Korea's rough terrain sometimes provided a false sense of security, promoting the belief that no major army could mount an effective attack under the difficult conditions posed by its natural obstacles.

That didn't stop other nations from trying, however, and invasions became more commonplace as new methods of warfare rendered natural barriers like mountains and oceans less effective. But navigating and dominating the peninsula was never easy for a foreign power. In fact, American general Douglas MacArthur's failure to fully understand Korea's terrain led him to make a disastrous decision that affected the course of the Korean War (see chapter four).

Buried Treasures

The mountainous lands of Korea do provide some significant benefits, however.

Geologists estimate that North Korea's mountains contain huge supplies of as many as two hundred different minerals, including iron, limestone, gold, graphite, zinc, copper, and tungsten. Some deposits may rank among the largest in the world.

Over the centuries, many countries—including Korea's neighbors as well as others from as far away as Europe and North America—wanted to either trade with or control Korea to gain access to these deposits. Japan, in particular, looked to the Korean peninsula to supply it with the raw materials it needed to modernize its factories in the latter part of the nineteenth century.

When the Korean peninsula was partitioned in 1945, most of Korea's mineral wealth wound up north of the dividing line. Today, despite its poor economy, North Korea may be sitting on as much as ten trillion dollars' worth of untapped riches lying under the surface of its extremely mountainous terrain.

Unfortunately, North Korea lacks the equipment, energy capacity, and resources necessary to mine, process, and export more than just a small fraction of its mineral wealth. In 2014, Russia offered to build a railroad line in North Korea in return for access to its mineral supply, but the plan was never finalized. Economic sanctions against North Korea—put in place by the international community in response to the country's continued development of nuclear weapons—have also made it difficult for North Korea to fully realize the potential of its natural resources.

In a June 2017 article published in *Business Insider*, author Chris Weller described North Korea's dilemma as it tries to take advantage of its mineral wealth:

> North Korea continues to face a catch-22 with its mineral stockpile. The country is too poor to use the deposits itself, but too volatile in its leadership to gain the trust of international bodies that may permit the minerals' export … The deposits will continue to sit underground, unused and untapped, until surrounding countries figure out a way to make workable partnerships.

While the partition awarded North Korea with plentiful resources, South Korea found itself cut off from many raw materials, forcing the country to turn to foreign trade and import the goods it needed to eventually become an economic powerhouse.

A NORTHERN ADVANTAGE

The partition of Korea didn't just divide Korean families; it also split up important natural resources, quickly pushing the economies of the north and south in two different directions.

After the Korean War ended in 1953, North Korean leader Kim Il Sung developed a series of economic plans designed to take further advantage of his country's mineral, forest, and fishing riches. North Korea's economy grew rapidly as manufacturing increased and the country began exporting minerals and manufactured goods to other countries, including Russia, China, Thailand, and even South Korea.

On the other side of the border, South Korea's economy lay in shambles after the war. Up until then, South Korea's people had relied mainly on agriculture, but the war had destroyed most of the farms and driven many families off of their land. South Korea had also depended on the minerals and forests of the north to supply raw materials and goods, but the war cut off South Korea's access to these important resources.

In the years since, South Korea has engineered a truly remarkable turnaround. The country has excelled in developing new industries, including technology and manufacturing, and now claims one of the world's strongest economies. On the other hand, North Korea has stumbled badly as a result of neglecting its economy in favor of its military and nuclear program.

Workers are pictured in a shoe factory in Wonsan, on the east coast of North Korea, in September 2017.

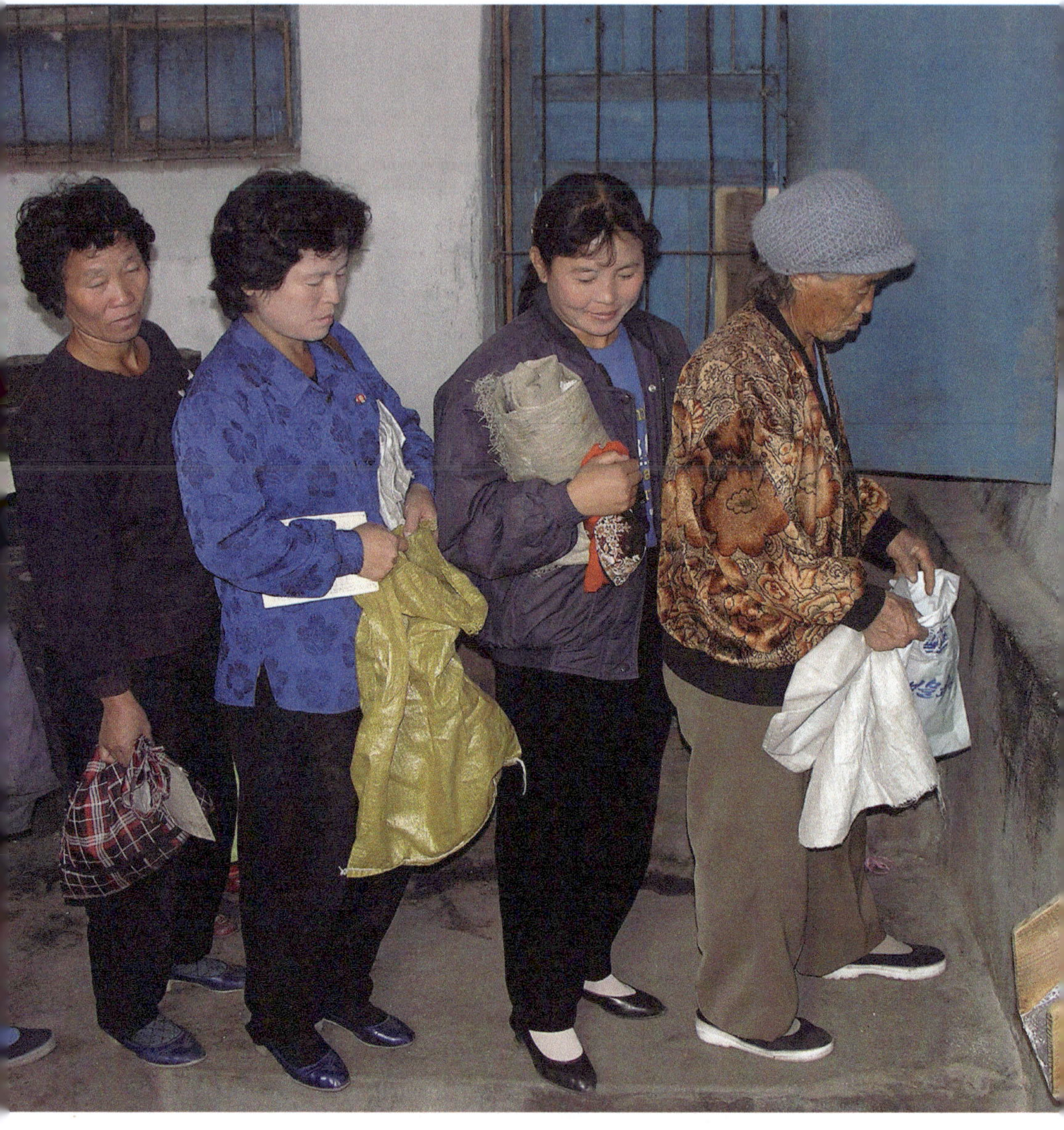

Food shortages occur often in North Korea, and its citizens sometimes have to stand in line to receive what they need to survive.

Food and Water

While North Korea's mountains may contain untapped mineral wealth of unknown proportions, the rough and rocky terrain leaves little room for farming. In fact, barely 22 percent of North Korea's land is suitable for raising crops and livestock, with much of that territory located in the vast plain near the western coast.

Unfortunately, the scarcity of good farmland makes it difficult for North Korea to produce enough food for its people. Shortages, starvation, and famine commonly occur in North Korea, and the country depends on importing food from other countries to fulfill its needs. Many countries have tried to use these food shortages to gain an advantage in negotiations with North Korea's hostile government.

While Korea's mountains can make farming and travel difficult, they also spawn many powerful and valuable rivers. Two longer rivers in the north help form the border between North Korea and China. The Yalu River flows west for 491 miles (790 km) to Korea Bay, while the Tumen River courses east for 324 miles (521 km) to the East Sea. The rivers separating North Korea from China became a major focal point during the Korean War when US and United Nations forces approached the border and China attacked in response.

Rivers played an important role in shaping early Korean life and contributing to the economy. With its mountains making travel by land difficult, Korea's rivers provided the means for transporting people and goods from one area to another. Korea's rivers also flow mainly north to south or east to west, and they eventually empty into the Yellow Sea or the Korean Strait, making rivers the best way to move goods to the coast for trade with other nations. Major cities such as Seoul in the south and P'yongyang in the north were originally built as ports along large rivers, and each city serves as its nation's capital today.

Rivers also provide water for drinking and irrigation, especially to the more plentiful farmlands of the south. Their strong flows have allowed Koreans to build massive dams that harness river currents, producing hydroelectricity and creating reservoirs.

The rules of real estate and "location, location, location" list oceanfront property as a valuable asset. Once again, the Korean peninsula offers that advantage. No part of Korea lies very far from the ocean. Throughout their history, Koreans have harvested much of their food and nutrients from the sea, and today fishing ranks as one of South Korea's major industries. The peninsula also boasts ports on its southern and western coasts that remain ice-free throughout the year.

DANGEROUSLY CLOSE

Seoul, South Korea's capital, lies only 35 miles (56 km) south of the DMZ. P'yongyang, the North Korean capital, sits about 90 miles (145 km) to the north of the border. Just 120 miles (193 km) separate the two cities from each other.

These outlets have proven to be attractive targets for countries like the Soviet Union, whose Pacific Ocean ports lie much further north and often cannot be used during the winter due to ice and harsh conditions. In the past, Russia also feared that Vladivostok, its only Pacific warm-water port (that is, a port that does not freeze in winter), could be vulnerable to Japan and Korea due to its location on the Sea of Japan. Controlling ports on Korea's west and southern coasts would minimize Russia's dependence on Vladivostok and provide clear access to the Yellow Sea and the Southern Pacific Ocean.

A Bridge and a Buffer

Regardless of its resources, nations have fought over the Korean peninsula for centuries simply to claim ownership of its spot on the map.

For thousands of years people have used bridges to make it easier to travel from one place to another over difficult terrain. While many of today's bridges have been constructed over obstacles like rivers or canyons, nature also provides its own bridges, stretches of land that have been used throughout history to connect people from all over the earth. For example, over many centuries, the Sinai Peninsula in the Middle East has served as a land bridge connecting Africa and Asia.

During the ice ages, Japan was actually connected to the continent of Asia by a similar land bridge, a natural strip of rocky land covered with mountains and volcanoes. Sea levels eventually rose to cover the land closest to Japan, but the remainder today forms the peninsula that we call Korea.

Time and time again, other nations have viewed the Korean peninsula as a bridge that linked one part of Asia with another. The bridge could be used for three different purposes: for trade; to invade other countries like Japan, China, or Russia; or as a buffer against attack from those same countries.

Even today, nations of the world view the Korean peninsula both as a strategic advantage and as a threat. North Korea still shares its border with China and Russia. At its shortest distance, parts of the peninsula lie less than 100 miles (161 km) from the Japanese mainland and from Vladivostok, Russia's major eastern port, and only 300 miles (484 km) from Shanghai in China. Korea could threaten Japan's access to the Pacific Ocean from the Sea of Japan and potentially interfere with China's access to the Yellow Sea. Simply put, none of the major nations of the world can afford to let the Korean peninsula fall into the hands of a rival.

Unfortunately, this reality played a large part in causing the partition of Korea in 1945. Since that time, the two Koreas have shared an artificial border, and Koreans have been forced to view their sisters and brothers across the dangerous DMZ and the 38th parallel with a combination of regret, hope, and fear.

North and South Korea as they are today, including important rivers and port cities, are pictured above.

CHAPTER FOUR

Division and Conflict

The end of World War II left the Allies victorious over Germany and Japan. However, the countries that had been united in battle now found themselves dangerously divided after the fighting ended, and this discord would lead directly to the partition of Korea.

Redrawing Korea After World War II

The Allies fell into two very different camps, based on their system of government and how they viewed individual rights. The United States, Great Britain, France, Australia, and other nations considered themselves to be free countries whose people chose their own leaders through elections. On the other side stood the Union of Soviet Socialist Republics (USSR, also called the Soviet Union). The USSR, a confederation of

The original partition line was drawn along the 38th parallel. The military demarcation line drawn after the Korean Armistice followed a slightly different route, highlighted in dark orange above.

several states including Russia, Belorussia, and Ukraine, had established Communist rule in the former Russian Empire in 1922 after a bitter civil war.

As the fighting ended, each side took steps to spread its views to the war-torn nations that had already suffered so much at the hands of Japan and Germany. One thing that both sides had in common, however, was their desire to avoid another war. Germany and Japan had finally been defeated, but millions of lives had been lost and many economies had been wrecked. The Allies hoped to avoid turning on each other so soon after their common enemies had been vanquished.

The situation was complicated by the fact that, at the height of their power, German and Japanese armies had attacked and occupied numerous nations around the world. Germany had absorbed many of the countries of eastern and western Europe; Japan had done the same in the Far East. American, British, and Soviet troops liberated these countries, pushing Germany and Japan back to their previous borders. Many of these battered nations now hosted Allied troops on their soil.

Even before their final triumph, the Allies anticipated that peace could present its own set of problems. The victorious nations would have to restore a sense of order to a world wrecked by war; governments would need to be reestablished, people resettled, cities rebuilt, and economies revitalized. The Allies would also have to decide the fate of Germany and Japan.

To work through these issues, the leaders of the United States, Great Britain, and the Soviet Union decided to meet. Two years earlier, in 1943, all three had traveled to Tehran, Iran, to develop strategies to win the war. They would now gather again to discuss how to best manage the peace that they were anticipating.

In February 1945, US president Franklin D. Roosevelt, British prime minister Winston Churchill, and Soviet premier Joseph Stalin met for a week at Yalta, a Russian resort city on the Crimean Peninsula. They knew that Germany's defeat in Europe was close at hand, but they feared that the Pacific war against Japan could drag on much longer.

Roosevelt and Churchill had two main goals to pursue at Yalta. First, they wanted to discuss the future of post-war Germany and eastern Europe. Second, they wanted to convince the Soviet Union to enter the war against Japan.

Trading Territory

Stalin was indeed interested in joining the war in the Pacific if it meant winning territory back from Japan that had been lost in the Russo-Japanese War. However, Stalin was more concerned about maintaining a buffer between his country and any future attacks by Germany and western Europe. Stalin's armies had expelled the Germans from eastern European countries, including Poland, Hungary, and Czechoslovakia. Now that the Soviets occupied countries that could provide the buffer he craved, Stalin was not about to give them back.

In the end, Roosevelt, Churchill, and Stalin agreed to demand Germany's unconditional surrender and

FDR, ARCHITECT OF NATIONS

Franklin D. Roosevelt (FDR) was first elected president of the United States in November 1932. Because there were no presidential term limits back then, Roosevelt was reelected three more times—in 1936, 1940, and 1944.

Roosevelt led the United States out of economic ruin and on to victory in World War II. He also helped lay the foundation for the United Nations. However, agreements that he and Great Britain made with the Soviet Union at the end of the war resulted in drastic, unforeseen consequences, including the partition of Korea and Soviet domination in eastern Europe.

Roosevelt first assumed office at the height of the Great Depression, the worst economic downturn in world history. Under his policies, which he referred to as the New Deal, the US government developed solutions to help businesses and banks recover their strength and bring relief to the American people. Several of his programs, such as social security, still exist in some form today.

When World War II first broke out in Europe, the United States tried to remain neutral. However, Roosevelt did send aid to Great Britain, France, Russia, and China to help them defend themselves against German and Japanese aggression. After Japan attacked the US naval base at Pearl Harbor on December 7, 1941, Roosevelt led the United States into war.

While FDR helped formulate the strategies that led the United States and its allies to victory in World War II, he also approved the policy that forced all people of Japanese descent who lived on the US West Coast to leave their homes and businesses and relocate to internment camps for the duration of the war. Today, many people believe that the internment of Japanese citizens violated their civil rights, and Congress awarded financial compensation to survivors in 1988.

In February 1945, Roosevelt attended the Yalta Conference in Crimea to meet with British prime minister Winston Churchill and Soviet general secretary Joseph Stalin and discuss how to manage the post-war world. In addition to setting the conditions for Germany's surrender, FDR and Churchill received Stalin's commitment to permit free elections in eastern Europe and to join the war against Japan. In return, Russia would get back territory it had lost in the Russo-Japanese War.

US president Franklin Roosevelt (*front, center*) met with Winston Churchill (*left*) and Joseph Stalin (*right*) at Yalta in 1945.

Two months after returning from the conference, Franklin D. Roosevelt suffered a massive cerebral hemorrhage and died on April 12, 1945. After the war ended, Stalin broke his promises and installed authoritarian Communist governments in eastern European countries including Poland, Czechoslovakia, Hungary, Romania, and Bulgaria. He also kept control of the northern half of the Korean peninsula.

While eastern European countries regained their independence after the dissolution of the Soviet Union in 1991, Korea still waits for unification.

planned to divide Germany amongst themselves after the war. Roosevelt and Churchill also allowed eastern Europe to remain under Soviet influence as long as Stalin promised to support free elections in the future. In return, Stalin committed to entering the war against Japan, for which he'd receive territorial concessions after Japan's defeat. Stalin also agreed to help Roosevelt found the United Nations.

As part of their discussions about the war in the Pacific, Roosevelt and Stalin agreed to establish an international trusteeship in Korea after the Japanese surrendered. However, they did not develop any specific plan for how that might be carried out. Tragically for Korea, Stalin's decision to enter the Pacific War and the lack of a plan to administer Korea afterward helped to seal the peninsula's fate.

Soviets in Korea

The Pacific War had already entered its final stages when the Soviets joined the fight against Japan. The United States had dropped the first atomic bomb on Hiroshima, Japan, on August 6, 1945. Two days later, on August 8, the Soviet Union declared war against Japan and launched an invasion of Manchuria and Korea. Meeting weak resistance, the Soviets quickly drove south down the Korean peninsula.

Even as the fighting continued, foreign powers were already thinking about how they might use the Korean peninsula to their advantage after Japan's defeat. The Soviet Union still wanted to control Korea so it could

Russian troops occupied the northern half of the Korean peninsula after declaring war against Japan in 1945.

use its warm-water seaports with direct access to the Pacific Ocean. A presence in Korea would also assure it a strategic position in southeast Asia close to Manchuria and China.

The United States, on the other hand, wanted to limit Soviet expansion and influence wherever it could. America also feared that the growing strength of Communism in China could make its way across the border, onto the Korean peninsula, and endanger still more countries nearby, including Japan.

Two Foreign Powers on Korean Soil

On August 9, the United States dropped a second atomic bomb, this time on the Japanese city of Nagasaki. Japan's surrender was imminent, but many of its soldiers and citizens remained on the Korean peninsula. The Allies now had to make plans to accept Japanese surrender when the time came. But how could that be arranged?

Korea's situation was more complicated than that of other countries that had been occupied by Japan or Germany during the war. These nations had been liberated by one army—either American or Soviet—not by both. In Korea, however, the Soviets had attacked the Japanese from the north, while the Americans were moving to control the peninsula from the south. When the war ended, Korea would host not just one "friendly" foreign force on its land, it would have two. Even worse, the countries that commanded these forces did not appear to be very friendly toward each other.

The Americans and the Soviets agreed that they'd accept the surrender of Japanese troops in Korea within the territory that each controlled. However, the borders of that territory still needed to be defined. The United States knew that the Soviet army had managed to take control of eastern Europe, and US leaders feared that the same thing might happen on the Korean peninsula.

Someone had to decide Korea's fate. Today, more than seventy years after the fact, it remains hard to believe how that decision was made.

Creating a Border

Dean Rusk would eventually serve as US secretary of state from 1961 to 1969 under Presidents John F. Kennedy and Lyndon Johnson. At the end of World War II, however, Rusk was an army colonel serving on General George Marshall's staff in the Pacific theater. In August 1945, Rusk and another officer, Colonel Charles "Tic" Bonesteel, were assigned to choose a dividing line for the Korean peninsula upon which both the United States and the Soviet Union could agree.

Rusk later wrote about their choice in his book, *As I Saw It*:

> During a meeting on August 14, 1945, the same day as the Japanese surrender, [Bonesteel] and I retired to an adjacent room late at night and studied intently a map of the Korean peninsula. Working in haste and under great pressure, we had a formidable task: to pick a zone

> for the American occupation. Neither Tic nor I was a Korea expert, but it seemed to us that Seoul, the capital, should be in the American sector. We also knew that the U.S. Army opposed an extensive area of occupation. Using a National Geographic map, we looked just north of Seoul for a convenient dividing line but could not find a natural geographical line. We saw instead the thirty-eighth parallel and decided to recommend that ... [Our commanders] accepted it without too much haggling, and surprisingly, so did the Soviets.

In his own words, Rusk realized that the 38th parallel "made no sense economically or geographically." What's more, the decision did not take into account any input from Koreans themselves regarding the placement of the border. However, Rusk reasoned, the situation was critical and they had to make a decision based on "military expediency."

No one at the time knew why the Soviets agreed so quickly to the US proposal. Perhaps Stalin did not want to provoke the United States by moving farther south. He also may have hoped to gain American concessions for other territory in Japan. In any event, just like that, the partition had been established.

Only Temporary

The border was not supposed to be permanent; the original intent was simply to set up a temporary dividing line between American and Soviet forces to determine who would accept the surrender of Japanese soldiers, and in what territory. The Russians would handle Japanese troops north of the line; the Americans to the south.

After the Japanese surrender, however, the United States and the Soviet Union both wanted to set up governments in Korea that were similar to those they had in their own countries. When the two countries could not agree on how to unite the peninsula, each side established a temporary government that reflected its own views—democratic in the south, Communist in the north. The United States then turned the responsibility of uniting the peninsula over to the United Nations (UN).

In the autumn of 1947, the UN General Assembly voted to support an election for all of Korea and to remove all foreign troops. The Soviet Union opposed the plan, however, and refused to allow UN observers to even enter the north. The UN decided to hold the election anyway in the only area where that would be possible: the US-controlled territory south of the 38th parallel.

Two Governments

On July 20, 1948, the Koreans south of the 38th parallel elected Syngman Rhee as their first president. The south's new Republic of Korea (ROK) was inaugurated under Rhee on August 15, 1948, and its capital city was established at Seoul.

Rhee, already in his seventies, had been one the student leaders of a group known as the Independence

Club that had campaigned in 1896 to expel foreigners, especially Japan, from the peninsula. After Japan colonized Korea, Rhee had lived in exile in the United States for forty years while campaigning for Korean independence. He also strongly opposed Communism.

Koreans in the north angrily reacted to the news of a separate election in the south by forming their own government. They modeled their Democratic People's Republic of Korea (DPRK) after the Soviet Union and established their capital city in P'yongyang. Kim Il Sung, a thirty-six-year-old former guerrilla leader during WWII who had trained in Russia and become a Communist, was chosen as their premier.

Both sides claimed to be the one true government of Korea, and both leaders stated their intention to unite the two halves of the country. The Russians recognized the new government of the north and withdrew their troops by the end of the year. US troops left South Korea just a few months after that.

The Korean War

In the years after World War II, the United States became increasingly concerned with the growing influence of Communism in the Far East. In January 1950, US secretary of state Dean Acheson outlined a policy for the defense of allies in the area against possible Communist aggression. While his plan encompassed Japan and the Philippines, it failed to include Korea and other countries. Acheson even went so far as to publicly state that "it must be clear that no person can guarantee these areas against military attack."

In retrospect, no one is sure whether the American failure to include Korea in its defense perimeter was simply an oversight or a strategic blunder. Regardless of the reason, the effects were swift and deadly.

North Korean premier Kim Il Sung noticed the apparent lack of US support for its Korean ally in the south, and he decided pursue his dream of unifying the peninsula under his rule.

Invasion

On June 25, 1950, the Korean People's Army (KPA) crossed the 38th parallel at 4 a.m. with ten divisions and one hundred thirty-five thousand men. South Korea's army was much weaker and not as well trained, numbering only eight divisions and about ninety-eight thousand troops.

At first, the United States and the Republic of Korea badly underestimated North Korea's strength, and also its intentions. American general of the army Douglas MacArthur had been a hero in World War II and now commanded all US and Allied forces in the Far East. When he first heard about North Korea's attack, he calmly stated, "This is probably only a reconnaissance in force … I can handle it with one arm tied behind my back."

The situation proved to be much worse. The North Korean forces soon overwhelmed the ROK army, and

South Korean's capital city of Seoul fell on June 28, just three days after the invasion began.

A Desperate Stand at Pusan

US president Harry S. Truman reacted quickly. He authorized US air and naval forces to support South Korea's army and decided to send US troops to halt the North Korean advance. He also asked the UN to help the United States and South Korea stave off the attack.

On July 7, the UN Security Council authorized the United States to lead a United Nations Command (UNC) force to fight back against the North Korean invasion. Sixteen nations sent soldiers to support the effort, but the United States supplied nearly 90 percent of the troops.

President Truman chose General MacArthur to lead the effort. MacArthur managed to move the American Eighth Army to Korea within two weeks, placing his troops in defensive positions to slow down the North Korean attack while avoiding any major battles. The general planned to "trade space for time" while he waited for additional UN forces to arrive.

US and South Korean forces soon found themselves driven south by the Communist onslaught, down to the very tip of the Korean peninsula, near the seaport of Pusan. While they managed to stabilize their position and halt the North Korean advance, their situation remained desperate.

General Douglas MacArthur (*right*) led US and UN forces against North Korean troops who invaded South Korea in 1950.

The Brilliant Offensive at Inchon

General MacArthur needed to come up with a plan not only to halt the North Korean attacks, but to put them on the defensive and push them back out of South Korea. What MacArthur chose to do next is still considered to be one of the boldest and most successful strategies ever used in warfare.

Rather than mount an offensive against the North Koreans near Pusan, MacArthur decided to launch an attack of his own on the other side of South Korea, well behind the North Korean forces. On September 15, 1950, MacArthur transported the Tenth United States Army by sea almost entirely around the Korean peninsula and landed his troops on the beaches at Inchon, located on the upper northwest coast near the 38th parallel. Inchon was already a port city and considered to be the gateway to Seoul.

MacArthur's amphibious assault came at great risk. If successful, US forces could trap the North Koreans between two US armies and perhaps even cut off their escape home. If it failed, it could mean terrible defeat and the loss of the entire Korean peninsula.

The move to the beachhead at Inchon turned out to be a great success. MacArthur did indeed catch the North Koreans between his two forces, and his soldiers wound up destroying more than two-thirds of the invading army. US and South Korean forces advanced inland and recaptured Seoul on September 27.

The United States' amphibious landing at Inchon surprised North Korean forces and turned the tide of the Korean War.

MacArthur then received the following orders: "Your military objective is the destruction of the North Korean armed forces. In attaining this objective, you are authorized to conduct military operations north of the 38th parallel in Korea."

The fateful decision to cross the border into North Korea triggered a chain of events with unexpected consequences that still haunt the Korean peninsula, and the world, today.

Escalation

At first, the counterattack across the 38th parallel seemed to be successful. US and UN forces quickly advanced north and swallowed up much of North Korea. The tattered North Korean army fell back in full retreat, and the reunification of the Korean peninsula appeared to be a real possibility.

As MacArthur continued his advance, however, he made a huge strategic blunder that turned out to be just as impactful as his brilliant landing at Inchon just one month earlier.

While he moved toward the northern border, MacArthur decided to keep his two armies separate. He sent the Tenth United States Army to the east, toward the Yalu River that divides the Korean peninsula from China. He sent his Eighth United States Army to the western edge of the Yalu, near the Chosin Reservoir. That left his forces divided, with the forbidding terrain of the T'aebaek Mountains separating his two armies.

US soldiers endured harsh winter conditions and bitter cold as they battled Chinese troops in North Korea.

MacArthur knew the geography of the area, but he based his strategy on two assumptions that turned out to be dangerously incorrect. MacArthur did not believe that any army could mount an attack from the T'aebaek Mountains because of its difficult terrain. He also believed that the Chinese would not get involved in the conflict and that, even if they did, his army could easily handle any new threat.

MacArthur was badly mistaken on both counts, and his miscalculation led to a severe escalation of the Korean War. The result? More years of bloody fighting and more suffering for the Korean people.

The China Factor

For more than one thousand years, China and Korea had shared a long and complex history across their border. At different times in their relationship, Korea had represented for China a source of resources, a trading partner, a bridge to further expansion, and a geographic buffer against foreign invasion.

China had been experiencing its own Communist movement since the early 1920s. Chinese Communist and nationalist forces had continued to fight each other even while they jointly battled Japan in World War II. After Japan surrendered, attempts to form a coalition government failed and, by 1946, China found itself engaged in a civil war.

Despite US support for Chinese nationalist leader Chiang Kai-shek, Communist forces under Mao Zedong finally triumphed in October 1949 and formed the People's Republic of China (PRC). The United States refused to recognize the new Chinese Communist state and suspended diplomatic relations with the Chinese mainland.

All that history now came into play as American and United Nations forces headed north toward the North Korean border—and Chinese territory.

While China and the Soviet Union now both called themselves Communist nations, their beliefs and practices differed to the point that they had become rivals rather than allies. When the Americans and the Soviets divided Korea after WWII, China resented the USSR's influence in a land so close to its own border. After Soviet troops left North Korea, China worked to increase its influence with its newly established Communist neighbor.

The North Koreans invaded the south in 1950 with support from both the Soviets and the Chinese. Now, North Korea itself was in danger of falling to democratic US and UN forces. Even more concerning to China, the fighting placed US forces close to China's own homeland.

In October 1950, the Chinese secretly sent four large armies into North Korea, positioning them in the T'aebaek Mountains between the two American armies. The space was narrow, only 20–50 miles (32–80 km) wide. In late November, the Chinese attacked MacArthur's two American armies at the Ch'ongch'on River in the west, and near the Chosin Reservoir in the east.

The fierce and unexpected Chinese attacks forced US forces to retreat. The Chinese now mounted their own offensive, driving south back past the 38th parallel.

On January 4, 1951, the Chinese briefly captured Seoul. Americans retook the city in March.

In the meantime, MacArthur began to publicly question his own government's strategy for Korea. He wanted to attack Chinese bases across the border, and perhaps even use nuclear weapons, but he felt that Washington, DC, was more interested in negotiation than in winning a military victory.

President Truman refused to allow MacArthur to cross into China. He did not want to further anger China, and he also believed that the Soviet Union might feel threatened by an expansion of the war so close to its own border with China and North Korea. On April 11, 1951, Truman replaced MacArthur with a new commander, Lieutenant General Matthew B. Ridgeway, who managed to halt the North Korean and Chinese advance and to push their forces back close to the original line along the 38th parallel.

Armistice, but No Peace

On July 10, 1951, the two sides finally met at Kaesong to begin peace discussions. The talks then moved to Panmunjom on October 25, but little progress occurred. For the next twenty-one months, the peace talks—and the killing—continued, with little political or military movement on either side.

Finally, on July 27, 1953, the opposing sides agreed to a cease-fire. After millions of deaths, untold destruction, and thirty-seven months of war, the two sides established a truce line very close to the original border that had been drawn after World War II. The Korean Armistice Agreement established the demilitarized zone (DMZ) and included an accord on how to exchange prisoners of war.

The Korean Armistice ended fighting between the two military forces in 1953. However, an armistice is not the same thing as a peace treaty, which needs to be discussed and agreed to by governments. The governments of North and South Korea never signed an official peace treaty and, even today, each side sometimes uses the absence of a formal treaty to justify provocations against the other.

The New Dividing Line

The armistice established a new dividing line—the military demarcation line, or MDL—between North and South Korea that closely matched the line across which the two sides had faced each other for the last two years of the Korean War. The MDL works its way about 150 miles (241 km) from east to west across the peninsula from the Sea of Japan (what Koreans call the East Sea) to Gyeonggi Bay on the west coast.

The cease-fire also established the demilitarized zone, or DMZ, a buffer measuring about 2.5 miles (4 km) wide that runs across the peninsula, along the MDL. Wire fences have been erected along both edges of the zone, and these are guarded on each side by troops from North Korea and the United

TWO FAILED ATTEMPTS TO UNIFY

The partition of Korea after World War II caused territory disputes that, in turn, led to the Korean War. When North Korean forces invaded South Korea on June 25, 1950, they moved south quickly before ROK and US forces managed to hold their position in the southeast corner of the peninsula near Pusan. After General Douglas MacArthur's brilliant attack behind enemy lines at Inchon, UN forces then pushed their way north and nearly reached the Chinese border.

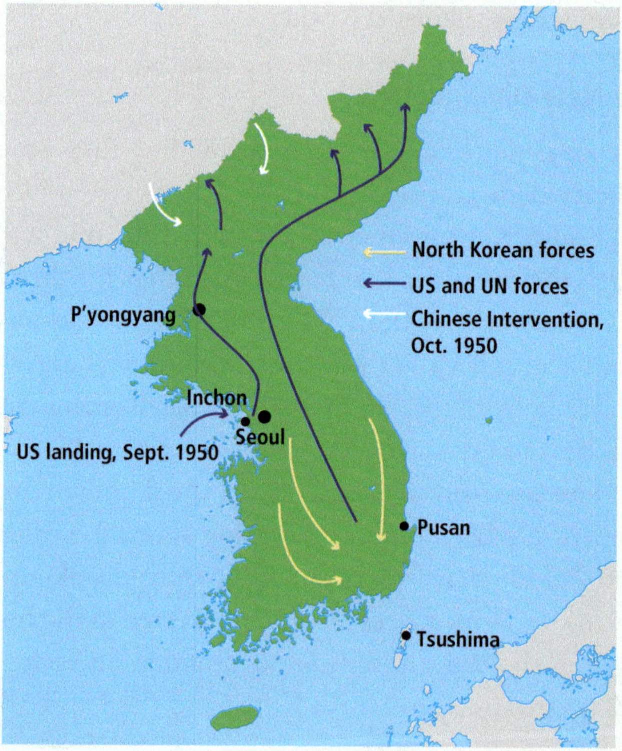

Korean, Chinese, US, and UN forces all criss-crossed the once-united Korean peninsula during the Korean War.

That October, North Korean and Chinese armies counterattacked and drove the UN forces back south toward the 38th parallel. Within the space of just a few months, both armies had nearly succeeded in uniting the Korean peninsula.

The next two years saw heavy fighting but little further movement. After the cease-fire in 1953, the new border between North and South Korea differed only slightly from the original line that had been drawn along the 38th parallel in 1945.

The Korean peninsula had endured three years of death and destruction for nothing.

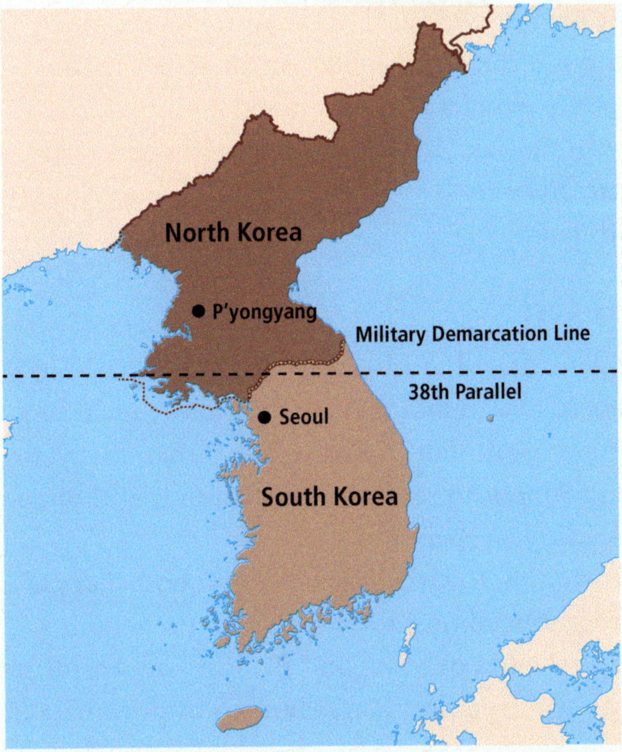

The border between North and South Korea as it is today was drawn in 1953, at the end of the Korean War.

A CONSTANT STATE OF WAR

A state of war still exists between South and North Korea. The armistice that ended the Korean War in 1953 instituted a temporary cease-fire "until a final peaceful settlement is achieved." However, no peace treaty was ever signed.

Nations Command, including South Korean and American soldiers.

The MDL is not the same line that divided the peninsula before the North Korean offensive in June of 1950. It's similar to the positions that opposing forces held for the last two years of the war, but it actually runs through the 38th parallel on an angle, starting south of the parallel in the west and ending north of the line in the east. Even so, people still often refer to the current border between North and South Korea as the 38th parallel.

A Heavy Cost

Both sides suffered terribly during the Korean War. In excess of two million Koreans perished, including more than one million civilians. More than thirty-six thousand American soldiers and six hundred thousand Chinese also lost their lives.

Many cities, towns, and villages on both sides of the border were almost totally destroyed, including both capital cities of Seoul and P'yongyang. Farmland throughout the peninsula was burned or pockmarked

Today soldiers from both sides stand guard along the barbed wire fence that marks the demilitarized zone (DMZ) between South and North Korea.

with craters from thousands of explosions, and most factories and businesses were obliterated.

Perhaps the worst atrocity of the war was how the Korean people acted toward each other. North Korea forced four hundred thousand South Koreans to join its army and executed many government workers, doctors, and educators whom it considered to be loyal to the south. For its part, South Korea executed an estimated one hundred thousand Koreans whom it believed to be Communists.

Sadly, the cruelty and bitterness between north and south has not abated since the armistice. In fact, the two sides today seem farther apart than ever.

CHAPTER FIVE

One People, Two Paths

If you were able to walk along the MDL today, you'd notice a series of small, yellow signs—1,292 in all—planted along its entire length. The sides of each marker contain the words "military demarcation line" written in two languages. The side facing south is written in Korean and English, while the side facing north is written in Korean and Chinese.

These rusting markers stand as a somber reminder that Koreans still share one common language, culture, and history. However, they now live in two societies that, in many ways, could not be more different.

Contrasting Leadership

After the Korean War ended, North and South Korea each chose a path that reflected the influence of their

More than one thousand bilingual signs trace the path of the military demarcation line (MDL) between the two Koreas.

occupiers immediately after World War II. North Korea took its cue from the Soviets and adopted Communism and a totalitarian government. South Korea chose to move toward democracy and capitalism with the support of its former occupier, the United States of America.

Korea's first two leaders after the partition came from similar backgrounds. North Korea's Kim Il Sung and South Korea's Syngman Rhee were both born in the north, and both fled Japanese occupation. Kim,

Kim Il Sung ruled the Democratic People's Republic of Korea (North Korea) from 1948 until his death in 1994.

however, went with his family to Manchuria and received political and military training from the Soviet Union. After becoming a Communist and fighting the Japanese during World War II, Kim returned to North

Syngman Rhee, the first president of the South Korean Republic, headed an authoritarian regime from 1948 to 1960.

Korea. In 1948, he became the first premier of the newly formed Democratic People's Republic of Korea, after which he assumed total control and ruled for forty-six years.

Rhee, on the other hand, relocated to the United States, where he lived for thirty years. He returned to Korea after World War II to promote immediate independence and unification of the peninsula, and when South Korea became independent in 1948, he became its first president.

Kim Il Sung portrayed himself as a god-like leader to be worshipped by all. He spied on citizens and used propaganda to control information and prevent anyone from questioning his authority. Images of "Great Leader" Kim Il Sung could be seen everywhere, and newspaper, radio, and television stories constantly extolled his wisdom and leadership. Kim cultivated support from fellow Communist countries, China and the Soviet Union, while remaining totally hostile to South Korea and the United States.

When Kim Il Sung died of a heart attack in 1994, his son, Kim Jong Il, took over as North Korea's "Dear Leader." After he died in 2011, his son, Kim Jong Un, succeeded him at age twenty-eight, making him the youngest head of state in the world. Since taking over, Kim Jong Un has sometimes proven even more aggressive toward his adversaries than his father and grandfather were, threatening to wage war against South Korea and to launch nuclear attacks against the US mainland. He has also ordered the executions of key political and military leaders in North Korea, including his own uncle.

Unlike North Korea, South Korea's current government is democratic and modeled very much on the United States'. However, it has taken many years to reach this state of stability. Syngman Rhee ruled with an iron fist for twelve years; at different times, he outlawed the opposition political party, executed an opponent for treason, and purged those who disagreed with him from the government.

Rhee was eventually forced to resign, but his departure did not end South Korea's political turmoil. In the years since, South Korea has experienced six republics, one revolution, and two coups as it moved toward the representative government we see today.

Two Philosophies, Divergent Paths

The differences between North and South Korea extend beyond their forms of government. When Kim Il Sung took control of North Korea, he introduced a philosophy of *juche*, or "self-reliance," meaning that North Korea wanted to manage its own affairs with no help or influence from outsiders. Mixing elements of Korea's traditional mistrust of foreigners with ideas taken both from Confucianism (proper behavior) and Communism (public ownership of property and, in the case of North Korea, obedience to the all-powerful government), Kim used juche to isolate his country, to the point where North Korea has now inherited the historical title of "Hermit Kingdom," by which the peninsula was known many decades earlier.

While the north instituted its policy of juche, South Korea created its own model for success. After

AN OCEAN BORDER

Since the Korean War ended, both North and South Korea have committed aggressive acts toward each other. Many of these incidents have occurred near the DMZ, where the North Koreans continue to dig tunnels in an attempt to infiltrate the south. Some of these incidents have turned violent, and more than six hundred people have died on both sides.

Not all disputes between the two Koreas have occurred on land, however. The waters off of Korea's west coast have also seen deadly conflict.

While the 1953 Korean Armistice clearly defined the land border between North and South Korea, the agreement did not draw any line dividing the oceans that lie off the peninsula's eastern and western coasts. In order to prevent any naval battles after the war, the United Nations Command gave South Korea control of five islands, known today as the Northwest Islands, and placed the ocean border between the islands and the North Korean shore. The border, known as the "northern limit line" (NLL), awarded valuable fishing grounds to South Korea. The area also controls important sea lanes that lead to ports on both the northern and southern Korean coast.

Although North Korea never recognized the NLL, it only began to dispute the border in 1973, when it started sending ships over the line. A 1991 agreement between North and South Korea seemed to settle the issue for a time, but in the late '90s, North Korea began to claim that the border should be moved farther south.

In 1999, a North Korean patrol boat violated the NLL but retreated after several sailors were killed in a gun battle. Three years later, six South Koreans died in a similar incident. In November 2009, South Korean navy ships attacked and quickly disabled a North Korean vessel that crossed the line.

Then, on March 26, 2010, the South Korean warship *Cheonan* exploded after being hit by a torpedo, killing forty-six sailors. Using evidence assembled by a team of international investigators, South Korea accused North Korea of attacking the *Cheonan* with its submarines, but North Korea denied any role in the incident.

Later that year, North Korea shelled Yeonpyeong, one of the disputed islands, in what it claimed was a reaction to South Korean military exercises near the border between the two nations' territorial waters. Since that time, the two sides have exchanged even more artillery fire.

South Korea has now heavily fortified Yeonpyeong, which lies only 6 miles (10 km) from the North Korean coast. One expert has called the NLL "the weakest link in the chain that holds the two Koreas from outright conflict."

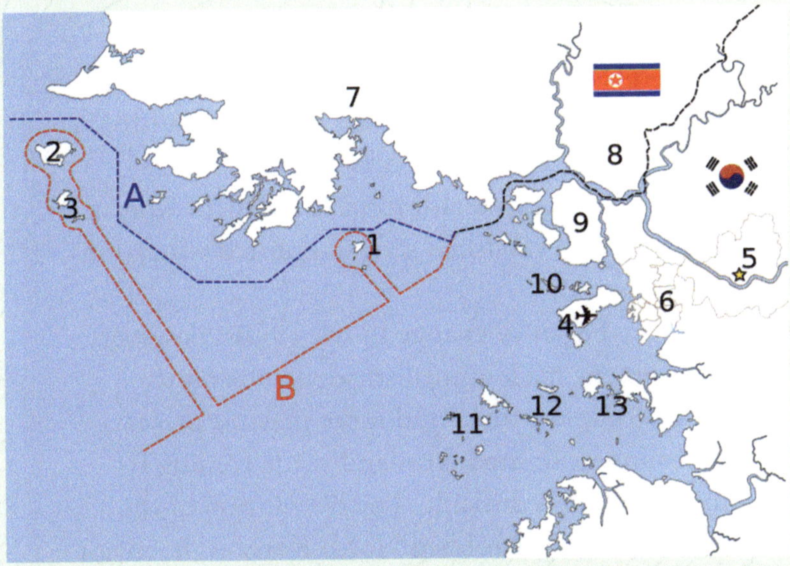

The northern limit line defines the ocean border between North and South Korea. This map shows key locations, including the islands of Yeonpyeong (1), Baengnyeong (2), Daecheong and Socheong (3), Yeongjong (4), Ganghwa (or Kanghwa) (9), Bukdo-myeon (10), Deokjeok-myeon (11), Jawol-myeon (12) and Yeongheung-myeon (13), as well as the cities of Seoul (5), Incheon (6), Haeju (7), and Kaesong (8).

the Korean War battered South Korea, its government tried to rebuild the economy by providing funds to businesses controlled by wealthy families, while protecting them from foreign competition. These businesses came to be known as *chaebol*, a term drawn from the combination of the Korean characters for "rich" and "clan." Well-known examples of chaebol include Hyundai, LG, and Samsung.

Chaebol helped South Korea become an industrial power, but they have also caused resentment among those Koreans who believe that chaebol wield too much influence and breed corruption in government and business.

North Korea: Economic Troubles

The economies of North and South Korea also moved in two different directions after the armistice. With help from the Soviet Union, Kim Il Sung used his country's vast mineral wealth to rebuild North Korean industry; he also established state-supported education and health care.

The story began to change in the 1970s, however. The government made unrealistic demands on its workers to complete more and more massive projects, and the country's limited farmland made feeding its growing population difficult. The dissolution of the Soviet Union in 1991 robbed North Korea of its major benefactor, leaving it more dependent than ever on China for both aid and international support.

Recently, North Korea's situation has continued to worsen as it commits more and more of its financial resources to its nuclear program and its army, leaving little money for investment in new and modern factories and products. As a result, North Korea's economy is languishing while its people continue to suffer.

Perhaps most striking, constant famine may be causing long-term physical problems for North Korean citizens. A recent study found that the average North Korean man stood one to three inches shorter than a typical South Korean male, and the World Bank estimates that North Koreans live twelve fewer years on average than those south of the border. In 2013, a United Nations report stated that 28 percent of North Korean children suffer from chronic malnutrition, while the World Food Program estimated that about 80 percent of North Korean families do not have enough important vitamins, proteins, and other nutrients in their diet.

South Korea: Economic Revitalization

For its part, South Korea has engineered a truly remarkable turnaround since the Korean War ended. Manufacturing has replaced farming, and today South Korea ranks as a world leader in the production of a diverse range of products, including steel, iron, automobiles, ships, and electronics; it also exports a great deal of seafood. In 2017, the International

Monetary Fund ranked South Korea's gross domestic product (GDP), which indicates a country's economic strength, among the top twelve in the world.

In large part as a result of political and economic differences, North and South Koreans lead starkly different lifestyles. While South Koreans enjoy all the technological advantages of modern life, fewer than one in ten North Koreans even own a mobile phone. The two countries even view time differently. South Korea follows the Gregorian calendar, the world's most widely used system, while sometimes referencing the older Korean calendar, such as in the case of traditional holidays. However, North Korea's official calendar is the juche calendar, which begins in 1912, the birth year of the country's first leader, Kim Il Sung, who cultivated a cult-like following. Therefore, in North Korea, the year 2019 is the juche year 108.

Despite their differences, both South and North Korea have periodically tried to reach out to explore better relations across the border. In 1971, the two sides agreed that their nations should become one and that the unification should be carried out peacefully and without undue influence from foreign countries. However, they could not agree on the framework for further talks, and the meetings ended suddenly in 1973. Any peace talks since then have always been clouded by

Opposite: According to CNN, Asian tourists regularly rank Seoul, the capital of South Korea, as their favorite world city.

어은미
한의원
Lee Eun Mi Korean Traditional Clinic
イウンミ韓医院
李恩美韩医院
3446-1240
牛里
Woorigarden
明洞 MART
明洞超市
明洞スーパーマーケット
MYUNG-DONG SUPERMARKET
Nine Tree
나인트리 호텔
유료 주차장
초가집
Milky Bee
$元 ¥€

PEACEFUL TRANSFORMATION

With the help of the United Nations Educational, Scientific and Cultural Organization (UNESCO) and other international groups, South and North Korea are working to transform the DMZ into a "peace park" that would protect and expand the wildlife and plants that have grown there since the Korean War.

one major issue: North Korea's insistence on developing nuclear weapons.

The Nuclear Threat

In August 1998, Kim Jong Il announced that building an economically and militarily powerful nation would become one of North Korea's most important goals, and it soon became obvious that nuclear weapons would play a key role. Kim knew that the free nations of the world would do anything to prevent North Korea from becoming a nuclear power, and he began to demand concessions and aid from other governments in return for limiting his country's development of nuclear weapons.

Since that time, North Korea has continued to play a dangerous game of nuclear "cat and mouse" with the rest of the world. In October 2002, North Korea terrified the globe by admitting it used fuel from a nuclear reactor to build nuclear bombs. In 2005, after two years of talks, North Korea agreed to halt its

North Korea's development of nuclear weapons continues to isolate it from the rest of the world.

weapons program in return for foreign aid. However, in October 2006, North Korea went back on its word and announced that it had successfully tested a nuclear weapon. Then, after again agreeing to halt its nuclear program in response to world economic sanctions, North Korea resumed its efforts and tested nuclear bombs in 2009 and 2013.

More recently, North Korea has tested missiles that could eventually carry nuclear warheads to Japan, other Asian countries, and even the US mainland. Today, North Korea's continued development of its nuclear program stands out as one of the most critical issues faced by nations around the world, and it continues to place the peninsula on the brink of war.

Torn Apart

It's true that discussions of governments, economies, social programs, and even nuclear weapons can help us understand the differences between North and South Korea. However, it is also important to remember that the tragedy of Korean partition affected the Korean people on a deeply personal level and that their pain continues today.

Koreans never expected their country to be divided, or for their country to be administered by foreigners after World War II; they wanted nothing more than to immediately reestablish their homeland. When foreign countries split the peninsula, Korean families were literally torn apart—husbands separated from wives, parents from children, sisters from brothers. Little did they know that their division would last more than seventy years, with no end in sight.

Painful Reunions

North Korea does not allow any communication between its citizens and the south, so most family members have received little news about relatives trapped across the DMZ after the war. Since 2000, however, North and South Korea have managed to arrange several reunions during which one or two hundred South Koreans have been allowed to cross the border and briefly meet with long-lost loved ones.

During a reunion in 2015, the *New York Times* described the heartbreak that partition had forced upon Korean families:

> As the husband she last saw 65 years ago hugged her on Tuesday, Lee Soon-kyu, an 85-year-old grandmother from South Korea, smiled shyly, like the young bride she once was.
>
> Ms. Lee had been married to Oh In-se for only seven months and was five months pregnant when the Korean War erupted in 1950. Mr. Oh disappeared into the conflict [and they] did not see each other again until Mr. Oh, now a deeply wrinkled 83-year-old, showed up wearing a black fedora …

Kim Hong-Kyun (*second from left*) was abducted and taken to North Korea in 1968. Here, he reunites with his eighty-eight-year-old mother (*right*) and his brother (*second from right*) in 2007. Korean families still suffer painful separation more than seventy years after their country was partitioned at the end of World War II.

> "I can't tell how much I missed you," said Ms. Lee, who never remarried and raised her son alone. "I have wept so much thinking of us that there are no tears left in me." …
>
> Ms. Lee said that after her husband appeared to her in a dream in 1978, she gave him up for dead and began holding an annual ritual for a deceased relative.

Since 1985, fewer than twenty thousand Koreans have been allowed to meet across the divide. Many who had hoped to once again see their loved ones have passed away, and most of those still waiting are now more than eighty years old.

Will Korean families ever be reconnected, and will the Korean people ever achieve their dream of one united people across the peninsula? Given North Korea's continued development of nuclear weapons and its threats against South Korea, the United States, and the world, it remains hard to believe that reunification will ever become a reality.

For now, the Korean people will be kept apart by an invisible, arbitrary line drawn by outside governments—a border created in order to settle a war whose consequences continue to haunt the Korean peninsula today.

CHRONOLOGY

- **108 BCE** The Chinese Han dynasty establishes four territories in what is modern-day Korea.
- **75 BCE** Koreans defeat the Han dynasty and establish the kingdoms of Silla, Koguryo, and Paekche.
- **668 CE** The Korean kingdom of Silla unifies the Korean peninsula.
- **918** Wang Kon founds Koryo.
- **1231** The Mongols invade Koryo.
- **1392** Yi Seong-gye establishes the New Choson dynasty.
- **1592** Japan invades Korea. It will invade again in 1597.
- **1598** Korea expels Japan from the peninsula.
- **1876** Korea opens three ports to international trade.
- **1894** China and Japan fight the Sino-Japanese War for control of Korea.
- **1895** Japan arranges the murder of Korean queen Min.
- **1905** Japan assumes control of Korea as a protectorate.
- **1910** Japan annexes Korea, marking the beginning of a thirty-five-year occupation.
- **1919** The March First Movement for Korean independence begins.

- **1941** Japan attacks Pearl Harbor, and the United States declares war.
- **1945** World War II ends. American army officers choose the 38th parallel to divide the Korean peninsula between US and Soviet forces.
- **1948** On August 15, the Republic of Korea is established in South Korea under President Syngman Rhee.
- **1948** On September 9, the Democratic People's Republic of Korea is established in North Korea under Premier Kim Il Sung.
- **1950** North Korea invades South Korea on June 25, triggering the Korean War.
- **1953** On July 27, North and South Korea sign an armistice to end the Korean War, and the demilitarized zone (DMZ) is established as the border between the two sides.
- **1971** North and South Korea hold reunification talks, which will collapse in 1973.
- **1972** Kim Il Sung becomes president for life in North Korea.
- **1976** Two US military officers are killed by North Koreans in the Joint Security Area of the DMZ on August 18.
- **1988** Seoul hosts the Summer Olympic Games.

CHRONOLOGY

- **1991** South and North Korea both join the United Nations. The collapse of the Soviet Union deprives North Korea of a major benefactor.
- **1994** North Korea's Kim Il Sung dies; Kim Jong Il assumes control.
- **1998** South Korean president Kim Dae-Jung begins talks with North Korea as part of a foreign policy approach, known as the "Sunshine Policy," aimed at improving relations between the two countries.
- **1999** Famine in North Korea kills millions.
- **2000** Some Korean families separated by partition reunite for the first time.
- **2002** North Korea admits that it has a secret nuclear program.
- **2003** Violating international agreements, North Korea continues nuclear development.
- **2006** North Korea test-fires long-range missiles and claims its first successful nuclear test.
- **2008** South Korean president Lee Myung-Bak ends the Sunshine Policy and adopts a hard line toward North Korea.
- **2009** North Korea announces its second nuclear test.

- **2010** Japan apologizes to South Korea for its aggression on the hundredth anniversary of the Japanese annexation of Korea. Tensions between North and South Korea increase after the sinking of a South Korean warship.
- **2011** North Korean leader Kim Jong Il dies; his son, Kim Jong Un, succeeds him.
- **2013** Kim Jong Un executes his uncle. North Korea conducts its third nuclear test.
- **2016** North Korea claims to have detonated a nuclear warhead.
- **2017** North Korea claims it has tested a hydrogen bomb and an intercontinental ballistic missile capable of reaching the US mainland, threatening a nuclear strike on the United States.
- **2018** South Korea hosts the Winter Olympics. North and South Korea choose to enter the opening ceremony together under a Korean Unification Flag. In women's ice hockey, they competed as a single team.

GLOSSARY

amphibious An adjective used to describe, in this case, a military attack on land launched from the sea.

annex To take control of an area of land or a country.

arbitrary Based on random choice rather than a specific reason.

armistice A temporary truce between warring parties.

austere Severe or strict in manner or attitude.

authoritarian Demanding complete obedience with no personal freedom.

catch-22 A frustrating situation in which someone is trapped by contradictory regulations or rules.

chaebol A large family-owned business in South Korea.

Communism The belief in an economic and social system in which property and resources are owned by a classless society instead of individuals.

Confucianism A system based on the teachings of the Chinese philosopher Confucius that stresses order, personal responsibility, and harmony.

cult A group of people living under the influence of an authoritarian, charismatic leader.

famine Extreme shortages of food.

homogeneous All the same kind; of common origin.

ideology A system of beliefs or practices.

Industrial Revolution The rapid development of industry that occurred in the late eighteenth and early nineteenth centuries, brought about by the introduction of machinery.

juche The concept of self-reliance introduced in North Korea in 1955.

parallel An imaginary line extending around the earth, parallel to the equator; it is used to indicate latitude.

peninsula A piece of land that juts out into water.

propaganda The art of spreading information, true or false, to make people believe a certain point of view.

protectorate A weak territory or country protected or partially controlled by another, stronger country.

sanction A penalty for disobeying a rule or law.

totalitarian Relating to a system of government that demands total obedience to the state.

tribute Payment made by one state or ruler to another as a sign of dependence.

UNESCO The United Nations Educational, Scientific and Cultural Organization, which encourages nations to cooperate through science, education, and culture.

United Nations An international organization of countries formed in 1945 to promote international peace, security, and cooperation.

FURTHER INFORMATION

Books

Berlatsky, Noah, ed. *North and South Korea* (Opposing Viewpoints). Farmington Hills, MI: Greenhaven Press, 2014.

Breen, Michael. *The Koreans: Who They Are, What They Want, Where Their Future Lies.* New York: St. Martin's Press, 1998.

Connor, Mary E., ed. *The Koreas* (Asia in Focus). Santa Barbara, CA: ABC-CLIO, 2009.

Halberstam, David. *The Coldest Winter: America and the Korean War.* New York: Hyperion, 2007.

Rice, Earl, Jr. *The Evolution of Government and Politics in North and South Korea.* Hockessin, DE: Mitchell Lane Publishers, 2015.

Websites

Demilitarized Zone (DMZ) Tours
http://english.visitkorea.or.kr/enu/ATR/SI_ENG_2_2.jsp

Visitors can arrange tours of all public sights inside and close to the demilitarized zone. The website includes detailed descriptions and histories of many different locations, as well as links to other information about Korea.

The Geography of the Koreas
https://asiasociety.org/education/geography-koreas

This website from the Center for Global Education at Asia Society includes a geographic exploration of the Korean peninsula, including its location, climate, economy, and how the Korean people perceive themselves.

North Korea
www.nti.org/learn/countries/north-korea

The Nuclear Threat Initiative monitors threats from nuclear, biological, and chemical weapons around the world. Its profile of North Korea includes details on the history and capabilities of the country's nuclear program.

Videos

Dramatic Video Shows North Korean Soldier's Escape Across Border
www.cnn.com/2017/11/21/asia/north-korea-defector/index.html

A video shows a North Korean soldier running across the military demarcation line in an attempt to cross the border into South Korea.

Inside North Korea | National Geographic
www.youtube.com/watch?v=TXYokXfbrWs

Correspondent Lisa Ling travels across the 38th parallel and into North Korea.

North Korea's Dangerous Border: Inside the DMZ [Pt.1] | Direct From with Dena Takruri
www.youtube.com/watch?v=a12yniZVGLQ

A visit to the demilitarized zone reveals how to enter the area and how it's managed, and offers background on the war that established the border as it is today.

BIBLIOGRAPHY

Armstrong, Charles K. "Korean History and Political Geography." The Center for Global Education at Asia Society. Accessed November 12, 2017. https://asiasociety.org/education/who-we-are.

Choe Sang-Hun. "South and North Korean Families, Separated by War 65 Years Ago, Reunite Briefly." *New York Times*, October 20, 2015. https://www.nytimes.com/2015/10/21/world/asia/south-and-north-koreans-separated-almost-a-lifetime-reunite-briefly.html?_r=0.

"Countries in the World by Population." Worldometers. Accessed November 10, 2017. http://www.worldometers.info/world-population/population-by-country.

Dubois, Jill, and Debbie Nevins. *South Korea* (Cultures of the World). New York: Cavendish Square Publishing, 2015.

Foran, Racquel. *North Korea* (Countries of the World). Minneapolis, MN: ABDO Publishing Company, 2013.

———. *South Korea* (Countries of the World). Minneapolis, MN: ABDO Publishing Company, 2013.

Fry, Michael. "National Geographic, Korea, and the 38th Parallel: How a National Geographic Map Helped Divide Korea." *National Geographic*, August 4, 2013. https://news.nationalgeographic.com/news/2013/08/130805-korean-war-dmz-armistice-38-parallel-geography.

Gifford, Clive. *North Korea* (Global Hotspots). New York: Marshall Cavendish Benchmark, 2010.

Hickman, Kennedy. "Russo-Japanese War: Battle of Tsushima." ThoughtCo, November 14, 2017. https://www.thoughtco.com/russo-japanese-war-battle-of-tsushima-2361199.

"Kim Il-Sung." *Encyclopædia Britannica*, August 22, 2017. https://www.britannica.com/biography/Kim-Il-Sung.

Kingsberg, Harold. "What Sparked Japan's Aggression During World War II?" *Slate*, July 7, 2014. http://www.slate.com/blogs/quora/2014/07/07/what_prompted_japan_s_aggression_before_and_during_world_war_ii.html.

"Korean War Fast Facts." CNN, June 10, 2017. http://www.cnn.com/2013/06/28/world/asia/korean-war-fast-facts/index.html.

"March First Movement: Korean History." *Encyclopædia Britannica*, Feb. 28, 2007. https://www.britannica.com/event/March-First-Movement.

McCurry, Justin. "Soldier Shot by North Korean Guards as He Defects to South." *Guardian*, November 13, 2017. https://www.theguardian.com/world/2017/nov/13/soldier-shot-by-north-korean-guards-as-he-defects-to-south.

"North Korea Nuclear Timeline Fast Facts." CNN, September 4, 2017. http://www.cnn.com/2013/10/29/world/asia/north-korea-nuclear-timeline---fast-facts/index.html.

O'Neal, Claire. *We Visit North Korea* (Your Land and My Land: Asia). Hockessin, DE: Mitchell Lane Publishers, 2014.

Pearson, James, and Ju-min Park. "The War That Never Ends Between the Koreas." Reuters, June 16, 2014. https://www.reuters.com/article/us-northkorea-islands-insight/the-war-that-never-ends-between-the-koreas-idUSKBN0ES00720140617.

Seth, Michael J. *A History of Korea: From Antiquity to the Present*. Lanham, MD: Rowman & Littlefield Publishers, Inc., 2011.

Somervill, Barbara A. *South Korea* (Enchantment of the World: Second Series). New York: Children's Press, 2015.

Sonneborn, Liz. *North Korea* (Enchantment of the World: Second Series). New York: Children's Press, 2014.

BIBLIOGRAPHY

"Syngman Rhee." *Encyclopædia Britannica*, August 10, 2016. https://www.britannica.com/biography/Syngman-Rhee.

Tejada, Carlos. "Money, Power, Family: Inside South Korea's Chaebol." *New York Times*, February 17, 2017. https://www.nytimes.com/2017/02/17/business/south-korea-chaebol-samsung.html.

Weller, Chris. "North Korea Is Sitting on a Stockpile of Minerals Worth Trillions." *Business Insider*, June 29, 2017. http://www.businessinsider.com/north-korea-stockpile-minerals-worth-trillions-2017-6.

"Yalta Conference." History.com, 2009. http://www.history.com/topics/world-war-ii/yalta-conference.

INDEX

Page numbers in **boldface** are illustrations.

INDEX

INDEX

INDEX

Gerry Boehme is a published author, editor, speaker, and business consultant who lives in New York. He loves to travel and learn about new things. Boehme has written books for students across a variety of subjects, including *Edward Snowden: Heroic Whistleblower or Traitorous Spy?*, *John Lewis and Desegregation*, and *Heresy: The Spanish Inquisition* (Public Persecutions). He has also spoken at conferences across the United States as well as in the United Kingdom, Australia, and the Republic of Korea, where he had the opportunity to visit the DMZ and talk with Koreans about the devastating effects of the partition of their country.